THE HISTORY OF THE FUJIWARA HOUSE

The monk Jōe 定恵 (643-666?) as depicted in the painting *Fujiwara no Kamatarizō* 藤原鎌足像, Muromachi Period. The Fujiwara patriarch features here as a Shinto deity, flanked by his two sons, the courtier Fuhito 不比等 (659–720) and the monk Jōe. Unfortunately, Fuhito's biography has been lost. Courtesy: Princeton University Art Museum.

The History of the Fujiwara House

A Study and Annotated Translation of the *Tōshi Kaden*

⌘

By

Mikaël Bauer
McGill University

LONDON AND NEW YORK

THE HISTORY OF THE FUJIWARA HOUSE
A STUDY AND ANNOTATED TRANSLATION OF THE *TōSHI KADEN*

First published in 2020 by RENAISSANCE BOOKS

Published 2025 by Routledge
4 Park Square, Milton Park, Abingdon, Oxon OX14 4RN
605 Third Avenue, New York, NY 10158

Routledge is an imprint of the Taylor & Francis Group, an informa business

© Mikaël Bauer 2020

All rights reserved. No part of this book may be reprinted or reproduced or utilised in any form or by any electronic, mechanical, or other means, now known or hereafter invented, including photocopying and recording, or in any information storage or retrieval system, without permission in writing from the publishers.

Trademark notice: Product or corporate names may be trademarks or registered trademarks, and are used only for identification and explanation without intent to infringe.

British Library Cataloguing in Publication Data
A catalogue record for this book is available from the British Library

ISBN: 9781912961184 (hbk)
ISBN: 9781912961290 (pbk)
ISBN: 9781003706502 (ebk)

For Product Safety Concerns and Information please contact our EU representative: GPSR@taylorandfrancis.com
Taylor & Francis Verlag GmbH, Kaufingerstraße 24, 80331 München, Germany

Contents

⌘

Acknowledgements	*vii*
Fujiwara Family Line	*ix*
Introduction	xi

Part I: Fujiwara no Nakamaro

• The Nara period	1
• The Fujiwara	3
• Fujiwara no Nakamaro	4
• Early life	7
• Political career	8
• Gradual rise to prominence	9
• The *Shoku Nihongi* entry for same date records	12
• The Rebellion	14
• Nakamaro's religious policies	17
• Nakamaro and *Tōshi Kaden*	19
• Scholarship on *Tōshi Kaden*	21

Part II: Narratives of the three extant chronicles

• The Chronicle of Kamatari	24
• The Chronicle of Jōe	28
• The Chronicle of Muchimaro	33

Part III: Translations

• The Chronicle of Kamatari	39
• The Chronicle of Jōe	63
• The Chronicle of Muchimaro	71
Bibliography	*91*
Index	*97*

Acknowledgements

⌘

MY TRANSLATION OF the *Tōshi Kaden* grew out of my doctoral research on the origins of Kōfukuji, the clan temple of the Fujiwara family. For this reason, I would like to start by thanking my academic advisor, Ryūichi Abe, and the members of my Ph.D. committee, Mikael Adolphson and James Robson. During several stays in Japan, I have always received much academic and personal support from Uejima Susumu and Robert Rhodes, who also read an earlier draft of my translations. At Kōfukuji in Nara I have always been welcomed by Gyoei.

Christopher Callahan, Andrea Pinkney and Meera Kachroo read the final draft and made valuable suggestions to improve the introduction and the prose of the translations. Richard Bowring kindly proofread the entire manuscript at its final stage. On various occasions I received valuable feedback and helpful suggestions from Ross Bender, Raji Steineck, Matthew Stavros and Thomas Conlan. At the School of Religious Studies at McGill I also enjoyed warm encouragement from Garth Green, Lara Braitstein, Hamsa Stainton and Rongdao Lai. Paul Norbury from Renaissance Books was very helpful and encouraging from the very beginning.

On a more personal level, I would like to thank first and foremost my parents: my father Raoul Bauer, an historian who has published widely on European history, and my mother Rita Van Camp, a retired teacher and art historian. Both have always encouraged my academic curiosity, although my topic of choice was quite distant from theirs. My sister Dominique Bauer has always been my best friend, showing interest in my work without fail. Finally I would like to thank my wife Yaxiang Lu, and her parents in China who always enquire about my work and teaching. Yaxiang has always been there for me, in Japan, the US, the UK and Canada and I am thankful for her love. Yuhan Peter and Yilin, my son and daughter, have always provided welcome and unwelcome distractions, both on and off the ice in Montreal.

Mikaël Bauer, Montreal
February 15, 2020

Fujiwara Family Line

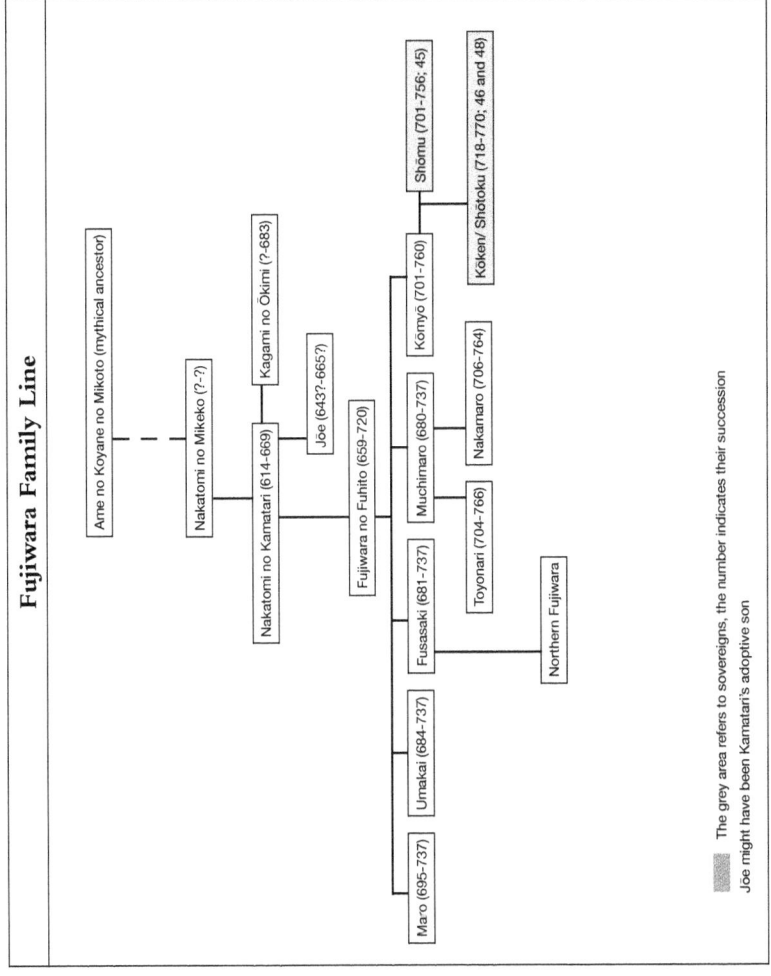

Introduction

⌘

THIS BOOK CONTAINS an introduction and an annotated translation of the eighth-century clan history *Tōshi Kaden* (藤氏家伝) or The History of the Fujiwara House. The text is attributed to the courtier Fujiwara no Nakamaro 藤原仲麻呂 (706–764) who, despite having been one of the most talented bureaucrats of the Nara period, was largely forgotten by later members of the Fujiwara clan given his reputation as traitor to the throne.[1] Passages from the imperial history *Shoku Nihongi* 続日本紀, or the chronicle *Wake no Kiyomaro den* 和気清麻呂伝, portray him as a shrewd individual whose sole purpose was to seize power at court and usurp the throne.[2] His 'rebellion' of 764 was one of several challenges facing the female sovereign Kōken 孝謙天皇 (718–770), two other examples being the Tachibana no Naramaro 橘奈良麻呂 (721–757) conspiracy of 757 and the infamous Dōkyō incident of 769.[3] However, as will be referred to below, the image of Nakamaro as traitor to the throne has been problematized by several Japanese and Western scholars.[4]

---

[1] Piggott, "Tōdaiji and the Nara Imperium", 64. Kishi, *Fujiwara no Nakamaro*, 293.

[2] Bohner, "Wake-no-Kiyomaro-den", 268. This text on the life of the eighth-century courtier Wake no Kiyomaro 和気清麻呂 (733–799) states the following (own translation): " In the eighth year of Hōji (764), the Great Protector (*taihō*) Emi no Oshikatsu (Fujiwara no Nakamaro) rebelled and was put to death. Three hundred of his followers were convicted...After his rebellion had ended, the people suffered and were famished" In other words, Nakamaro caused the people to suffer. *Wake-no-Kiyomaro-den, GR* Vol. 5, 354.

[3] Throughout this monograph, the translation 'emperor' for 'tennō' 天皇 has been avoided. Instead, 'sovereign' is used.

[4] See for example Nakanishi, *Shoku Nihongi to nara chō no seihen*, 211. Kimoto summarizes that often Nakamaro is portrayed as (own

The History of the Fujiwara House comprises three biographies: the *Kamatari den* 鎌足伝 (The Chronicle of Kamatari), the *Jōe den* 定慧伝 (The Chronicle of Jōe), and finally the *Muchimaro den* 武智麻呂伝 (The Chronicle of Muchimaro). A fourth part, the *Fuhito den* 不比等伝, is referred to at the end of Kamatari's chronicle but has unfortunately been lost.[5] What follows is not a comprehensive analysis of the foundational period of the Fujiwara clan, but provides an introduction and translation of a text that will contribute to a better understanding of the politics and culture of eighth-century Japan.

Other better known historical sources, such as *Kojiki* 古事記, *Nihon Shoki* 日本書紀 or the *Rikkoku shi* 六国史, are, of course, central to the study of the early history of the Japanese court and the emergence of the Fujiwara clan, but *Tōshi Kaden* is important because it contains passages and details not found elsewhere. Not only does *Tōshi Kaden* help us to reconstruct the political and cultural context of its period, it also urges us to reflect on East Asian intertextuality and, more specifically, it shows the degree to which the drive to represent the Fujiwara family as inseparable from the line of sovereigns relied on continental rhetoric.[6] *Tōshi Kaden* clearly borrows from *Nihon Shoki* but also uses many references and quotations from continental histories. In his research on the imperial poetry collection *Man'yōshū* 万葉集, Torquil Duthie has pointed out that the late seventh-century

---

translation) 'Someone who ruled arbitrarily, used sovereign Junnin as a puppet, opposed Kōken and died as a traitor (*gyakuzoku* 逆賊) on the shores of lake Biwa'. Kimoto himself disagrees with this characterization. Kimoto, "Fujiwara no Nakamaro shōron, ritsuryō kanryōsei kokka to senken izoku no shōmetsu", 77. Bender also refers to Kimoto's analysis, stating that it was in fact Kōken, and not Nakamaro, who started the military events. Bender, *The Edicts of the Last Empress*, 31.

[5] Fukuyama speculates that parts of the Chronicle of Fuhito are included in one of the oldest sources pertaining to the history of the Fujiwara temple, Kōfukuji 興福寺, the *Kyūki* 旧記. Fukuyama, *Nihon kenchiku shi kenkyū*, 332. He also indicates it as having been authored by Nakamaro.

[6] Hasebe Masashi, "Fujiwara no Nakamaro to Tōshi kaden", 179.

Japanese court was represented as a realm 'under Heaven,' borrowing extensively from Chinese sources and imagery: the Japanese (or rather 'Yamato') court 'aspire[d] to the ideal of a universal realm ruled by a universal ruler.'[7] Japanese histories borrowed terminology, imagery and at times whole passages from various Chinese sources such as the *Huainanzi* 淮南子, *Yijing* 易経, *Chunqiu* 春秋 (relying on the *Chunqiu gongyang zhuan* 春秋公羊伝 commentary, that discussed such matters as dynastic change, abdication and its moral implications) and the *Shiji* 史記.[8] In 757, Nakamaro issued an order in which the study of several Chinese classics was clearly stated, showing how he saw the organization and implementation of the study of history was essential to the construction of a strong state.[9] In the process, he added several texts that were extra to the normal requirements.[10] As pointed out by Evgeniya Sakharova, over twenty Chinese historical works are quoted from in Jōe's biography alone, showing the pervasive influence of continental literature on the Japanese court around this period.[11]

---

[7] Torquil Duthie, *Man'yōshū and the Imperial Imagination in Early Japan*, 1.

[8] Go, "*Nihon shoji to shunjū kuyō den*", 2–3. Gentz describes how this text itself became a form or ritual expression, showing that the composition and reading constitute in themselves a ritual performance. Gentz, "The Ritual Meaning of Textual Form", 128–134.

[9] The word 'order' here refers to a document called 'choku' 勅, in this case issued in Tenpyō hōji 1 (757).11. The edict specifically mentions the texts to be studied by students (生) divided into the following categories: the classics (経生), history (伝生), medical works (医生), acupuncture (針生), astronomy (天文生), Yin-yang (陰陽生), and calendric works (暦竿生). These works had to be studied by the students of the Daigakuryō 大学寮, an academy for training officials. See Enomoto, "Fujiwara Nakamaro seiken ni okeru tō bunka no juyō", 20. Of note in relation to the *Tōshi Kaden* and sources referred to therein, is that the history works in this decree refer to three categories (large, middle and small), and that passages of several of these occur in the Kaden. See also Bender & Lu, *Research Note, a Japanese Curriculum of 757*, 1–3.

[10] Enomoto Jun'ichi, "Fujiwara Nakamaro seiken ni okeru tō bunka no juyō" 20–23.

[11] Sakharova, "Fujiwara House Biography: Continental prototypes", 82.

Composed a few decades after the first imperial histories, *Tōshi Kaden* emphasizes the ideal of the moral minister, while *Kojiki* and *Nihon Shoki* take the sovereign and the unbroken succession of monarchs as their main focus.[12] As explained by Duthie, in *Nihon Shoki* it is the sovereign who is the 'organizing subject that defines the historical field.'[13] This is fundamentally different in the text attributed to Nakamaro. In *Tōshi Kaden*, the focus shifts from the monarch to the minister, forging two seemingly unbreakable connections: one between the Fujiwara and the monarch, and one between Nakamaro and his forebears.[14] The metaphor describing the Fujiwara as the sovereign's 'wings' (*yoku* 翼), illustrates well this unbreakable bond between Kamatari's lineage and the sovereign. This bond is also emphasized by the depiction of Fujiwara officials as ideal Confucian *junzi* (君子), an image that runs through all three biographies. Indeed, Kamatari, faced with the events of the Taika rebellion of 645 at the Yamato court, is often compared to those servants from Chinese history who helped establish a new dynasty, more specifically during the Zhou (1122 BCE–221 BCE), Han (206 BCE–220), and Tang periods. *Tōshi Kaden*, composed at a time when Nakamaro himself faced substantial opposition at court, clearly reflects the political situation of the mid eighth century.[15] Here, the very act of honouring the patriarch Kamatari is on the one hand illustrative of the still unstable, fragile power of the Fujiwara after the 730s, but also presents a good example of

---

[12] Duthie, *Man'yōshū*, 117. The *Kojiki* and *Nihon Shoki* were composed in 712 and 720 respectively.

[13] Duthie, *Man'yōshū*, 129.

[14] This metaphor refers to several passages from the *Tōshi Kaden*, where the Fujiwara are described as wings protecting the sovereign or the realm. In the Chronicle of Jōe we read: "So erudite and benevolent, wings protected our policies." In the Chronicle of Muchimaro we find: "As feathers and wings of the emperor he gently stroke all under heaven." For the Japanese of these passages, see *TK* 281 and *TK* 392 respectively.

[15] It is also worth noting that the Chinese examples Kamatari is compared to are all prior statesmen, while the Korean examples from Silla mentioned in the text are his contemporaries. Sakharova, "Fujiwara House Biography: Continental prototypes", 84.

how the mid-eighth century Fujiwara sought to receive privileges as descendants of the successful events of 645.[16]

It is significant to note that the relation between Nakamaro and his great grandfather, the Fujiwara patriarch, Kamatari, is portrayed as the transfer of morality itself.[17] We are lead to conclude that Kamatari possessed qualities that became engrained in the Fujiwara bloodline. The following passage from The Chronicle of Kamatari illustrates well how the Fujiwara servant presents himself to his sovereign as an example of morality, describing how Prince Naka no Ōe 中大兄皇子 questions the moral dimension of their intention to kill the courtier Iruka without the consent of the sovereign. The text reads:

> Naka no Ōe : "How can the Principle of the subject be in accordance with Righteousness?"
> The Great Minister Kamatari: " The actions of her subject consist of Loyalty and Piety.[18] The Way of Loyalty and Piety unifies the country and brings prosperity to the clans. To allow for the sovereign's line to be cut off and allow for its foundations to be shattered and destroyed…It is not filial and not loyal to not proceed with our action."

Given Nakamaro's own intention to 'rebel' at the height of his power at court, a situation that will be explained below, the parallel created between him and his patriarch is inescapable. As illustrated by several passages, *Tōshi Kaden* could be considered to be a counter narrative to the official court histories and draws our attention towards a more inclusive understanding of Nara period literature. It is indeed limiting to interpret this period's histories, poetry and artistic expression merely from the imperial point of view. In The Chronicle of Muchimaro, the Fujiwara official is portrayed as the embodiment of morality: he retreats to the

---

[16] Togashi, "Kanshin no keifu", 1–2.
[17] See also Yen-Yi Chan, "The Kōfukuji Nan'endō and its Buddhist Icons: Emplacing Family Memory and History of the Northern Fujiwara Clan, 800–1200", 86.
[18] 'Her' refers to Kōgyoku 皇極天皇 (594–661), Naka no Ōe's mother (in other words the parent of two later sovereigns, Tenji and Tenmu).

mountains and the countryside and exercises 'non action' (*wuwei* 無為).¹⁹ It is also he and not the sovereign, who climbs a mountain and gazes over the landscape, performing a *kunimi* 国見 ritual that was usually the prerogative of the sovereign. As Ebersole explains, the ritual act of *kunimi* not only aims to request peace and good harvest to the land: the act reflects back on the ruler, showing the power and legitimacy of the sovereign.²⁰ In this case, however, it is Muchimaro who is given these qualities.

Rather than merely celebrating the patriarch, *Tōshi Kaden* aims to achieve two objectives that had important political repercussions. First, it portrays the Fujiwara as the sovereigns' main servants; an unbreakable connection formulated with terminology and examples borrowed from various Chinese sources. Second, it reinforces Nakamaro's own lineage, that of the Southern Fujiwara, and can be seen as an attempt to justify his own position as the Fujiwara's highest official.²¹ In this sense, the text connects authority and power: the composition of *Tōshi Kaden* and poetry, or the ability to change the calendar, only belonged to those who held the highest authority at court. Nakamaro's sponsorship of history writing clearly transcends the mere 'recording' of history: through the usage of specific passages from various Chinese histories, *Tōshi Kaden* 'educates' and illustrates rather than simply records. For example, in addressing the plot to assassinate Soga no Iruka, the text states:

大臣具述撥乱反正之謀²²

---

¹⁹ For research that questions the exclusively 'imperial' character of eighth-century poetry anthologies, see for example Ethan Bushelle, "Mountain Buddhism and the Emergence of a Buddhist Cosmic Imaginary in Ancient Japan," 1–36.
²⁰ Ebersole, *Ritual Poetry and the Politics of Death in Early Japan*, 25.
²¹ Togashi, "Kanjin no keifu: toshi kaden ni okeru gunshinkan to sono tokushitsu", 1–2.
²² *TK*, 69. The expression '撥乱反正' is rendered by Okimori as '乱を撥め反を正す' (*TK*, 151), an order not followed in the GR, where 反 functions as the verb. Thus, the statement could also be translated as 'to quell disorder and return to the normal', which basically means the same as in Okimori's rendering; *GR*, 342.

The Great Minister stated in detail the plot to eliminate disorder and return to the correct way.

This phrase 'to eliminate disorder and return to the correct way' (撥乱反正) is in fact paraphrased from the *Chunqiu gongyang zhuan*, and is also found in the Records of the Grand Historian and The History of the Han (*Hanshu*) where it is used to describe the justification to unify the realm.²³ The *Gongyang zhuan* contains historical narratives, ritual rules, and exegetical texts.²⁴ While the text contains several topics, one of its main objectives can be found at the beginning of its first part: the unification of rule or *da yitong* (大一統).²⁵ In Nakamaro's time, 'unity' at court was certainly at risk given the gradual escalation towards military conflict in 764. This influence of the *Chunqiu gongyang zhuan* on the narrative of The Chronicle of Kamatari will be discussed in due course.

---

²³ The phrase 撥亂世, 反諸正, 莫近諸 ("For bringing order to chaotic times, for making things right again…(*the text continues*: nothing can approach the efficacy of the Spring and Autumn Annals) " appears in the *Chunqiu Gongyang zhuan*'s chapter on Ai Gong, year 14; The *Records of the Grand Historian* mentions this concept in its chapter on Emperor Gaozu. See Miller trans., *The Gongyang Commentary on The Spring and Autumn Annals*, 276. Go, "Nihon shoki to shunjū kuyōden", 1.

²⁴ Gentz, "Long Live the King, The Ideology of Power between Ritual and Morality in the Gongyang zhuan", 5.

²⁵ Gentz, "Long Live the King", 8. This 'unification' in the *Gongyang zhuan* might refer to the unification of Qin and Han empires.

Part I

Fujiwara no Nakamaro

⌘

The Nara period

JAPAN'S NARA PERIOD (710–794) has often been described in terms of stability, the creation of 'state Buddhism' (*kokka bukkyō* 国家仏教), or the establishment of the country's first permanent capital, *Heijō-kyō* (平城京). All too frequently, however, it is forgotten that this was, in fact, a turbulent period in which political strife, bloodshed, uprisings and religious struggles featured prominently. It was a culturally vibrant century, with the construction and sponsorship of some of Japan's most famous temples and shrines, such as the foundation of Kōfukuji in 710 at the new capital, or Tōdaiji's dedication in 745. In addition, it was the century of Japan's most famous female sovereign, Kōken 孝謙天皇 (718–770), daughter of Shōmu 聖武天皇 (701–756) and 'Imperial Consort' Kōmyō 光明皇后 (701–760). Her edicts in the court chronicle *Shoku Nihongi* (続日本紀) reveal a horizon of meaning consisting of Buddhist elements, 'kami' (神) worship and Chinese notions of kingship.[1]

Central to this early, emerging Japanese state, was the rise of the Fujiwara family, undoubtedly pre-modern Japan's most illustrious aristocratic clan. Originating in the Nakatomi family (*Nakatomi*

---

[1] Ross Bender, trans., *The Edicts of the Last Empress, 749–770: A Translation from Shoku Nihongi*, 5. Kōken was the last female sovereign of the classical period, it would take until the Edo period for two female sovereigns to appear. Ross Bender, "Changing the Calendar: Royal Political Theology and the Suppression of the Tachibana Naramaro Conspiracy of 757," 224.

uji 中臣氏), their descendants would occupy most of the court's highest ranks for centuries, and names such as Fujiwara no Michinaga 藤原道長 (966–1027) would become synonymous with the culture of the Heian period (794–1185).

Of particular relevance to the compilation of *Tōshi Kaden*, the Nara Period was one in which there was significant borrowing from the continent in both religious and institutional terms. Not only did the Japanese court send embassies to China and the Korean kingdoms on a regular basis, monks, bureaucrats and artisans from the continent also travelled to Japan. In the seventh century, Japan sent no less than ten missions to the Tang court, where the Japanese took their place amongst representatives from other tributary countries.[2] The Japanese court and its sovereign clearly modelled themselves after the Chinese example, and formulated their role in no less sacred terms.

When the female sovereign Suiko 推古天皇 (554–628) died, an unstable period ensued, with an increasing role for members of the Soga clan. Following several conflicts, mainly involving Soga no Iruka (whose murder is described in *Tōshi Kaden*), Kamatari and prince Naka no Ōe were able to defeat the Soga in 645, Naka no Ōe ascending the throne as Tenji in 668. When Tenji died in 671 another conflict over the succession arose, resulting in the Jinshin wars (*Jinshin no ran* 壬申の乱), as a result of which Tenji's brother Tenmu became sovereign in 673. Strife between these two lines would continue for many years, not resolved until 770, when Kōnin 光仁天皇 (709–782) became sovereign, to be followed by Kanmu 桓武天皇 (737–806), both from the Tenji line. These dynastic struggles involved much violence, as illustrated by Tenmu's killing of Tenji's son and crown prince Ōtomo, his own nephew, in 672. Tenmu's own line would end violently as well, when Kōnin eliminated his nephew Crown Prince Osabe.[3] The Fujiwara were central to these disputes.

□

---

[2] von Verschuer, *Across the Perilous Sea*, 3–4.
[3] Ooms, *Imperial Politics and symbolics in Ancient Japan*, 2–4.

The Fujiwara

Historically, the Fujiwara had their roots in the Nakatomi family, and passages from both *Nihon Shoki* and *Kokiji* connect them not only with the birth of the line of sovereigns but also with the creation of the Japanese islands themselves. In one iconic passage, the Sun Goddess Amaterasu locks herself into a cave, plunging the world into darkness. The Fujiwara's divine ancestor, *Ame no Koyane no Mikoto* 天児屋根命, plays an important role in luring her out of the cave and restore light over the world.[4] From myth into history, the Nakatomi/Fujiwara thus seem to have been present from the beginning of times. Their origins are also addressed in later sources such as the following scene from the Kasuga scrolls, an elaborate *emaki*, picture scroll, dating back to the Kamakura (1185–1333) period. "When Amaterasu pushed open the Celestial Rock Cave, she illumined the darkness that had engulfed the world…This means that she and *Ame no Koyane no Mikoto* are conjoined in profound union…"[5] *Nihon Shoki* explicitly explains this deity as being the 'ancestor of the Nakatomi no Muraji.'[6] In other words, the Fujiwara and the line of sovereigns are always mentioned in the same vein, and their unbreakable union is emphasized from the beginning.

As we see from The Chronicle of Kamatari, Tenji conferred the name 'Fujiwara' on the dying Nakatomi no Kamatari in 669.[7] Kamatari thus became the family's patriarch

---

[4] As mentioned by Hardacre citing Ebersole, the cave scene might refer to the ritual of double burial of a sovereign. *Ame no Koyane no Mikoto* might thus represents the Nakatomi, participating in a ritual to 'recall' the soul to the body. Hardacre, *Shinto*, 53–54.

[5] Abridged from Royall Tyler, *The Miracles of the Kasuga Deity*, 161. Grapard also stressed the connection between the Nakatomi and this deity, mentioning that Nakatomi no Kamatari worshipped this god and his consort Himegami. See Grapard, *The Protocol of the Gods: A Study of the Kasuga Cult in Japanese History*, 23–24.

[6] Aston, *Nihongi*, 1:42. NS, *kamiyo ue*,116–117.

[7] According to the *Nihon Shoki*, Tenji sent his younger brother to Kamatari's residence to confer upon him the name 'Fujiwara.' See Aston, *Nihongi*, 2:291; NS, Tenji 8 (669).10.15.

and the new family name was continued through his eldest son Fuhito 藤原不比等 (659–720).[8] The Fujiwara's ascent to power was not an immediate event, however, but rather a gradual process that reached its height during what is called the 'Period of Regents' (*sekkan jidai* 摂関時代), from the tenth through the twelfth centuries. While Kamatari holds tremendous prestige, it was his son Fuhito who laid the real basis for early Fujiwara power. Within a few years of Fuhito's death, three of his sons were members of the Great Council of State (*Daijōkan* 太政官), and from 726 to 737 the Fujiwara's control of the court was firm.[9]

As might be expected, the Fujiwara themselves were hardly a homogenous group. There were four main branches, of which the 'Northern Fujiwara' (*Fujiwara hokke* 藤原北家), sometimes also referred to as the 'Regent's line', became the most powerful. The compiler of at least part of *Tōshi Kaden*, Nakamaro, Kamatari's great grandson, belonged to the Southern line, and the narrative is therefore aimed at establishing the authority of the Southern lineage, which was eventually eclipsed by the Northern line. Nakamaro was defeated in a military conflict in 764 and was consequently labelled a traitor. As a result of his downfall, he is given a bad reputation in *Shoku Nihongi*, where his institutional reforms and his political career are dismissed. His contributions to the growth of Buddhism, the development of the court bureaucracy, or his influence in literature and the arts have for this reason been largely overlooked.

□

Fujiwara no Nakamaro

Reading through passages from the *Shoku Nihongi* related to the events of 764, it is clear that Nakamaro is seen as a traitor

---

[8] Originally all of Kamatari's descendants received the name, but in the eighth month of 698 it was decreed that only Fuhito was allowed to keep the name 'Fujiwara.' See Chan, "The Kōfukuji Nan'endō and its Buddhist Icons," 28. Takashima, *Fuhito*, 272.

[9] Piggott, "Tōdaiji and the Nara Imperium," 49.

to both court and sovereign. Following a fierce military conflict with then Retired Sovereign Kōken, he was executed along with about thirty of his close family members and followers.[10] The entry for the twentieth day of the ninth month of 764 reads:

> The rebellious and dirty wretch Nakamaro with deceitful, twisted intent raised troops in order to overthrow the court...[11]

The text continues in the same vein:

> ...we realized that Nakamaro's heart was wicked and treacherous. The memorials he offered up previously were all lies and flattery...[12]

Since the *Shoku Nihongi* was written by his adversaries, we should keep in mind that the conflict of 764 was more complex in nature than just the rebellion of a courtier who wanted to usurp power, and, as argued by Kimoto, the clash between Nakamaro and Kōken cannot simply be reduced to a conflict between 'imperial power' and 'governmental' power as has often been done.[13]

When Nakamaro and his elder brother Toyonari 豊成 (704–766) were still of modest rank, Fujiwara domination was threatened by the rise of the courtier Tachibana no Moroe 橘諸兄 (684–757), and it was only with the help of his aunt, the Imperial Consort Kōmyō, did he attempt to regain the upper hand.

In addition to Nakamaro's so-called rebellion of 764, the figure of the Buddhist monk Dōkyō (道鏡; ?–772) has given

---

[10] The *Shoku Nihongi* contains edicts issued by Kōken, but its compilation as one history started in 794 during Kanmu's court. Sakamoto, *The Six National Histories of Japan*, 90–91.
[11] Bender, *The Edicts of the Last Empress*, p. 86; *SN*, Tenpyō hōji 8 (764).9.20.
[12] Bender, idem, p. 86; *SN*, Tenpyō hōji 8 (764).9.20. Kimoto, *Nakamaro*, 307.
[13] Kimoto, *Fujiwara no Nakamaro shōron*, 86.

rise to much speculation. In the popular imagination and several introductions to Japanese history, he is mainly portrayed as the monk who seduced the female sovereign. Following a famous oracle from the Hachiman Shrine in Kyūshū in 769 he was prophesied to become sovereign himself. However, after another oracle dismissed this, he disappeared from the higher levels of power after Kōken's death.[14] Of modest background and without notable achievements before his rise, Dōkyō had been one of Nakamaro's main opponents. After the rebellion, in 764, he was appointed Great Meditation Master *Daijin zenshi* (大臣禅師), and in 766 he was elevated to 'Dharma King' (*Hōō* 法王), a position created for him.[15] As stated by Bender in his work on Kōken/ Shōtoku's edicts, later Heian period sources represented her as a weak, female sovereign at the mercy of this 'villainous' monk, a version of the facts that since long has been the official interpretation of the so-called 'Dōkyō incident'.[16] However, Joan Piggott already pointed out that Dōkyō, from common descent, owed everything to Shōtoku and was only put in charge of Buddhist affairs through her volition. In other words, instead of Dōkyō controlling policy, this might well be seen as an attempt by Shōtoku to control the Buddhist community.[17] After Shōtoku's death in 770, Dōkyō was quickly removed and banished to Shimotsuke province where he later died.[18]

□

---

[14] By that time, Kōken had ascended the throne for a second time as sovereign Shōtoku. Bender, "The Hachiman Cult and the Dōkyō incident", 125–126; Bender, "Hachiman", 973.

[15] Following the appearance of a relic at Sumidera, Kōken (by then again the sovereign as 'Shōtoku') issued an edict celebrating the Dharma (Buddhist teachings) and conferring the rank of 'Dharma King' on Dōkyō. Bender, *The Edicts*, 98–101; *SN* Tenpyō jingo 2 (766).10.20; Kimoto, *Fujiwara Nakamaro*, 308.

[16] Bender, *The Edicts*, 5–6.

[17] Bowring, *Religious Traditions of Japan*, 95. Ambros, *Women in Japanese Religions*, 50–51.

[18] Piggott, "Tōdaiji and the Nara Imperium," 77–78.

Early life

Born around 706, Nakamaro was the second son of Fujiwara no Muchimaro and grandson of Fujiwara no Fuhito.[19] Not much is known regarding his early youth, and neither is the identity of his mother confirmed, although the *Kugyō bunin* states that he and his older brother Toyonari shared the same mother.[20]

The entry in the *Shoku Nihongi* for the year 764, as part of his eulogy, refers to him as being an intelligent and learned man.[21] At the time of his birth, when the capital was still located at Fujiwara-kyō, his father Muchimaro, Fuhito's eldest son, held the position of Head of the Academy (*daigaku no kami* 大学頭).[22] *Shoku Nihongi* describes that as a child Nakamaro studied under Abe no Sukunamaro 阿部少麻呂 (?–?), perhaps revealing a close link to the Abe family through his mother's side.[23] The same passage includes the well-known description that Nakamaro's 'nature was sharp and intelligent, and he was well read.'[24] The Chronicle of Muchimaro does not mention this, however, and seems to suggest that Muchimaro taught his sons. Given that Muchimaro was put

---

[19] No records exist confirming the date of his birth; some place his birth in 710 but there seems to be consensus about the year 706 as the *Kugyō bunin* mentions he died at age 59 in 764.
   Kimoto, *Fujiwara no Nakamaro seiken no kisoteki kōsatsu*, 1. See also Kishi, *Fujiwara no Nakamaro*, 8–9.

[20] Kimoto, *Fujiwara no Nakamaro*, 4; Kishi, *Fujiwara no Nakamaro*, 9. It is suggested by both Kimoto and Kishi that his mother belonged to the Abe clan.

[21] *SN*, Tenpyō Hōji 8 (764).9.18.; Kimoto, *Fujiwara no Nakamaro seiken*, 2. It is suggested that his mother was a daughter of Abe no Sadahira 阿部貞吉(?–?). The Chronicle of Muchimaro mentions that Muchimaro's sons were raised by a daughter of Sadahira, and it is assumed that she must have been their mother. Kimoto, *Fujiwara no Nakamaro seiken*, 4. The *Kugyō bunin* adds that Nakamaro and Toyonari had the same mother; Kishi, *Fujiwara no Nakamaro*, 9.

[22] The Chronicle of Muchimaro mentions he held this position. Kishi Toshio, *Fujiwara no Nakamaro*, 8.

[23] Kimoto, *Fujiwara no Nakamaro seiken*, 4–5; Kishi, *Fujiwara no Nakamaro*, 11. *SN*, 305.

[24] The *SN* contains the phrase 率性聡敏 in his eulogy, *SN* Tenpyō hōji 8 (764).9. See also Kimoto, *Fujiwara no Nakamaro*, 2.

in charge of the Academy at age thirty, it is certainly possible that he was qualified enough to do so.[25] According to *Shoki Nihongi*, Nakamaro entered the Academy as lesser attendant (*daigaku no shō jō* 大学少允) in 726, a position he took on after having been palace attendant (*udoneri* 内舎人).[26] Given the important position Fuhito held, it is probable that the young Nakamaro was promoted mainly because of the influence of his grandfather, rather than through the efforts of his own father.

☐

Political career

Initially, Nakamaro's career followed a gradual pace, always placed under his older brother Toyonari.[27] Unsurprisingly, in the early stages of his career, hierarchy demanded that he always stay behind his father and older brother in court rank. One year after Great Minister of the Right (*udaijin* 右大臣) Fuhito passed away, Muchimaro was promoted to Middle Counsellor, (*chūnagon* 中納言).[28] As Fuhito's eldest son he was bound to move up to the highest positions and in 734 he finally reached the rank of Great Minister of the Left (*sadaijin* 左大臣).[29] During these fourteen years Nakamaro's progress was gradual and his path did not change significantly until his father died in 737.[30] Muchimaro was fifty-seven years old at the time and perished in a smallpox epidemic that swept the country, killing up to one fourth of the population, including his three brothers Fusasaki 房前 (681–737), Umakai 宇合 (694–737) and Maro 麻呂 (695–737).[31]

---

[25] Kishi, *Fujiwara no Nakamaro*, 16.
[26] Kimoto, *Fujiwara no Nakamaro seiken*, 6; Kishi, *Fujiwara no Nakamaro*, 19–20.
[27] Kishi, *Fujiwara no Nakamaro*, 21–22.
[28] *KB*, Yōrō 5.
[29] *KB*, Tenpyō 6.
[30] *KB*, Tenpyō 9.
[31] Farris, *Japan's Medieval Population: Famine, Fertility, and Warfare in a Transformative Age*, 9; Kimoto, *Fujiwara no Nakamaro: sossei wa satoku kashikoku shite*, 15.

The 737 epidemic turned the composition of the Great Council of State on its head and resulted in Tachibana no Moroe, who otherwise held the lower rank of *sangi* (参議), quickly moving to the position of Middle Counsellor and eventually *dainagon*. Moroe had no real competition, the only Fujiwara on the Great Council of State being Nakamaro's older brother Toyonari. Several groups formed, however, resulting in a complex web of factions. Moroe became central to an anti-Fujiwara group along with members from the Ōtomo, Saeki and Agata-Inukai families, while Sovereign Shōmu and Imperial Consort Kōmyō formed a powerful counter-block. The descendants of the four deceased Fujiwara elders competed among each other and against Moroe. The most famous direct result of these tensions was the short-lived revolt by Fujiwara no Hirotsugu 藤原広嗣 (?–740), Umakai's disgruntled son, who rose against Moroe, targeting his close supporters the Hossō monk Genbō 玄昉 (?–746) and Kibi no Makibi 吉備真備 (695–775), only to be killed after his forces brought from Dazaifu in Kyushu were defeated by those of the central government.[32]

☐

Gradual rise to prominence

It is not certain when Nakamaro caught Kōmyō's eye or why she preferred him to Toshiyori, who was several years ahead of his younger brother in terms of appointments. It is suggested that from an early stage both brothers had quite different talents, with Nakamaro being skilled in the letters and bureaucracy, while Toshiyori appears to have been more skilled in military matters. Most likely, their father Muchimaro assigned them different career routes from very early on.

In 743, Nakamaro was appointed to the Great Council of State as *sangi* or 'counsellor' when he received the upper vice fourth

---

[32] Kimoto mentions that the court was able to raise roughly 17,000 men, while Hirotsugu's forces numbered around 10,000. Kimoto, *Fujiwara no Nakamaro*, 25; Kishi, *Fujiwara no Nakamaro*, 77–78.

rank (從四位上), the same year his brother was appointed to the much higher position of Middle Counsellor.[33] Both brothers had made steady progress in the previous years, but Nakamaro advanced at a slower rate until 743. But Moroe, Kibi no Makibi, and the monk Genbō still blocked his path. The first step towards challenging Moroe's grip on state affairs was Nakamaro's appointment as Minister of Ceremony (*Shikibukyō* 式部卿, a position that allowed him to select bureaucrats himself and thus provided him with the opportunity to place allies at strategic posts, such as the promotion of his younger brother Otomaro 乙麻呂 (737–760) to the military position of *Hyōbu no daifu* (兵部大補).[34] Within a year Nakamaro was in a position to challenge Moroe. Perhaps nothing illustrates his newly-acquired authority better than his ability to order that the Chinese characters for Yamato be changed back to the original (倭国), undoing a change that Moroe had instituted.[35] Things rapidly changed in his favour when Retired Sovereign Genshō 元正天皇 (680–748) died in 748 and Shōmu abdicated the next year, leaving the throne to his daughter, Kōken. Genshō had not been of Fujiwara stock and had supported Tachibana no Moroe until her death.[36]

Nakamaro was soon promoted to the high position of Dainagon, only to find that Moroe promoted his own son to the Great Council of State that same year.[37] To circumvent this move, Kōmyō and Nakamaro came up with the ingenious strategy of founding the new office of *Shibi chūdai* 紫微中台 in 749.[38] Nakamaro became head of this office, *Shibi naishō* 紫微内相 in 757.[39] As pointed out by Piggott, Nakamaro here demonstrated his political talent: he understood that the sovereign could govern

---

[33] *KB*, Tenpyō 15; Kimoto, *Fujiwara no Nakamaro: sossei wa satoku kashikoku shite*, 37.
[34] Kimoto, *Fujiwara no Nakamaro*, 25.
[35] Moroe had changed the name into 大養徳, also read ' Yamato no kuni'. Kimoto, *Fujiwara no Nakamaro*, 16.
[36] Naoki, "The Nara State," 259–260.
[37] *KB*, Tenpyō hōji 2.
[38] Kimoto, *Fujiwara no nakamaro: sossei wa satoku kashikoku shite*, 63–64. This office found its origins in Kōmyō's Imperial Consort's Office.
[39] *SN*, Tenpyō hōji 1 (757).5.20.

directly by edict, the only thing that was needed was a process allowing promulgation and implementation of edicts without the approval of the Great Council of State.[40] The Imperial Consort now started issuing orders (*choku* 勅) approved by the *Shibi chūdai*.[41] This arrangement seemed to have worked perfectly until Kōmyō's death in 760. In the long run, it was the loss of her support that seems to have signalled the gradual decline of Nakamaro's own position.

After this appointment, Nakamaro proceeded to introduce far-reaching institutional reforms that deeply affected the organization of the state on the one hand and the internal structure of the temples on the other. *Shoku Nihongi* mentions that Nakamaro drafted an Order of Five Articles (*choku go jō*) on 757/6/9. The text mentions the following measures. First, the heads of all the uji were not allowed to assemble their members at will. Second, no one could exceed his breeding quota for horses. Third, arms quota were put into place. Fourth, apart from official guards, no one was allowed to bear arms within the capital. Finally, in the capital no more than twenty horses could be assembled.[42] It is clear that these five measures are directed against a possible military uprising in the capital, a point of action undoubtedly related to military disturbances and unrest during the preceding years, such as the incident involving Tachibana Naramaro.

757 marks the start of the height of Nakamaro's influence at court and during that year he initiated several institutional reforms. First, it was the year in which he promptly enforced the *Yōrō ritsuryō*, a legal corpus originally promulgated by his grandfather Fuhito, replacing the *Taihō ritsuryō* of 701, a set of legal texts that formed the basis of the ritsuryō state till then. Second, he donated land for the organization of Kōfukuji's Yuima-e (or 'Vimalakīrti Assembly'), thus claiming headship of the Fujiwara house. A memorial granting land originally belonging to Kamatari

---

[40] Piggott, "Tōdaiji and the Nara Imperium," 62–63.
[41] Matsuo, *Tenpyō*, 278. Hayashi, *Kōmyō kōgō*, 172. *KB*, Tenpyō shōhō 9. Matsuo states that Nakamaro was selected by Kōmyō to head the office. Matsuo, *Tenpyō no seiji to sōran*, 278.
[42] *SN*, Tenpyō hōji 1 (757)/6/9; Kimoto, *Fujiwara no Nakamaro: sossei wa satoku kashikoku shite*, 91–92.

to the support of the Yuima-e but not mentioning Kamatari's illness as the origin of the ritual, was issued on 757/8/17:[43]

> As for the Vimalakīrti Assembly today held at Yamashinadera, it was founded by the Great Minister of the Interior, Kamatari. The foundational vow slipped away, changed, and for thirty years people did not come together and celebrate; the Assembly was discontinued. Thereupon, when the Fujiwara family arrived at court, the Head of the Council of State Inshi, Fujiwara no Fuhito, was distressed that the Lecture Hall was about to fall in decline and sighed that the temple had not yet been completed. Thus, he issued a Great Vow pursuing to continue prior actions. Thereupon, the marvellous assembly started to be held each year in the winter, on the tenth day of the tenth month. On the commemorative day of the Great Minister of the Interior the lecture took place to protect the imperial house, to maintain the Law of the Buddha, to guide their spirits to the way of the Buddha, and to encourage the diligent students of the Buddha.

The *Shoku Nihongi* entry for the same date records:

> He humbly vowed to donate merit fields to the temple for eternity to support the Vimalakīrti Assembly, so Maitreya will make it flourish and that for all times the dedication ceremony for the Great Minister of the Interior shall be held, that Heaven and Earth are in union and its transmission may be long, that the eminent voice of the imperial consort may be heard, that sun and moon might be together and shine from afar.[44]

As a third act, Nakamaro created the position of abbot or *bettō* (別当) at Kōfukuji, the first to be appointed to this position being *Shō sōzu Jikun* 慈訓 (691–777), a monk of common background who seems to have been instrumental in several of Nakamaro's policies as regards the Buddhist community.[45] Nakamaro's appointment of Jikun as abbot could be considered a turning point in his attitude towards the Buddhist community's internal structure.

---

[43] *SN*, Tenpyō Hōji 1 (757)/8/17.
[44] Own translation, *SN*, Tenpyō Hōji 1 (757).8.17.
[45] *KBS*, 1. Miyazaki, *Nihon kodai no shakyō to shakai*, 164.

This involvement was not limited to Kōfukuji however, as he was also close to Rōben 良弁 (689–774), Tōdaiji's first abbot from 752 to 760.[46] Another example of a monk he kept close was Gangōji's Chikō 智光 (709–781).[47] When Junnin was enthroned as sovereign in 758, Nakamaro received the honorary name *Emi no Oshikatsu* (恵美押勝) and became Great Protector (*taiho* 太保) or de facto Great Minister of the Right.[48] The same day, he issued an order regarding a change of bureaucratic titles, which reflected Tang-period designations of government offices. The adaptation and assimilation of continental institutional developments requires separate study, but in relation to Nakamaro it is worth briefly mentioning two elements. First, Nakamaro's implementation of Tang court ranks mirrored the situation in other areas of Chinese influence, in Silla, for instance.[49] Second, it is important to note that we are dealing with Tang-style nomenclature; the actual role of the office might differ.[50] Nakamaro's implementation of Tang court titles is obviously connected with his role in the study curriculum for bureaucrats, and the borrowing of ideas from several Chinese histories as seen in the *Tōshi Kaden*.

Kishi has pointed out that Nakamaro was in fact asked to compose an official history to follow after *Nihon Shoki*,[51] and that that Nakamaro's implementation of the Yōrō codes in addition to this historiographic project highlight his efforts to connect his persona with Fuhito's. However, *Nihon kōki* 日本後紀 states that Nakamaro's work contained too many mistakes and the work was never

---

[46] Nagamura, *Chūsei tōdaiji no soshiki to keiei* ,27.
[47] Kimoto, "Fujiwara no Nakamaro no bukkyō seisaku to sōgō", 54.
[48] *KB*, Tenpyō hōji 2. On Tenpyō Hōji 2 (758).8.1, Kōken instructed that an appropriate honorific for Nakamaro be found. On Tenpyō Hōji 2 (758).8.25, he received the title of Great Protector (*taiho* 太保). See Bender, *Nara Japan, 767–770: A Translation from Shoku Nihongi*, 77 and 84.
[49] Kochi, "hendō no yochō" , 103.
[50] Sakaue, "The Comparative Study of the Ritsuryō Bureaucracy in Ancient Japan and Tang China", 20. Bender, *The Edicts of the Last Empress, 749–770*, 29.
[51] Kishi, *Fujiwara no Nakamaro*, 306.

completed.⁵² Nevertheless, the fact that Nakamaro was involved with the creation of a history in relation with his institutional reforms, and the composition of his own clan history reveal the extent of his authority at court and his desire to connect with the power of his forebears.

□

The Rebellion

Initially Nakamaro's position and collaboration with Kōmyō continued without incident but this changed when his patron passed away in 760.⁵³ Nothing symbolizes better the break between Nakamaro and Kōken (who at the time held the position of Retired Sovereign) as the edict of 762 in which she limited Junnin's responsibilities to ceremonial matters and stated that she herself would take care of the 'matters of state.'⁵⁴ This edict was not in fact directed towards the sovereign but to Nakamaro. Despite Kōken's efforts, Nakamaro persisted and militarized his influence to protect Junnin's position. There is some dispute as to whether he was merely clinging to his own power or trying to 'protect' the sovereign, but they are not mutually exclusive. Nakamaro now depended on being Junnin's minister and for this reason protecting the monarch indirectly implied safeguarding his own position. Some historians, such as Seki, have posited that

---

⁵² As cited by Kishi, *Fujiwara no Nakamaro*, 304. Bentley translates this passage from the *Nihon kōki* as 'There is much rice and salt (i.e. many trivial details), but important events are missing'. Bentley, "The Birth and Flowering of Japanese Historiography", 64.
⁵³ Matsuo, *Tenpyō no seiji to sōran* , 279.
⁵⁴ Matsuo, *Tenpyō no seiji to sōran* , 281. Bender translates the key sentence in the edict of 762 (Tenpyō Hōji 6.6.3) as follows: " ...Junnin has not obeyed Us reverently...He has spoken wrongfully in Our name... Now as for the government, the Mikado will carry out the small duties of the usual ceremonies. We shall carry out the fundamental duties of the great things of state." Bender, *The Edicts*, 85. The term 'great things (of state)' refers to the concept *daiji* 大事, a term also used in the *Tōshi Kaden* and borrowed from Chinese sources.

the eighth-century state basically consisted of two conflicting poles that attempted to enlarge their influence: the power of the monarch versus the power of the nobility.[55] One could therefore also argue that the composition of one's clan history, and the sponsorship of temples and shrines, illustrates the struggle between these groups.

Nakamaro's position seems to have taken a dramatic turn for the worst on 964/9/11. Following the enforcement of several imperial sanctions issued by Nakamaro, Kōken sought for a way to undermine their legitimacy and therefore had the royal bell and seal taken from Junnin's palace.[56] Nakamaro immediately took action and dispatched his son Fujiwara no Kusumaro 藤原順儒麻呂 (?–764) who attacked Yamamura no ō 山村王 (?–?) and managed to retrieve both the bell and seal. Residing at her convent Hokkeji, Kōken immediately ordered Sakanoue no Karitamaro 坂上苅田麻呂 (728–786) and Oga no Shimatari 牡鹿嶋足 (?–783) to retaliate. In the ensuing battle, Kusumaro was killed by Shimatari. Nakamaro then sent his subordinate Yatabe no Oyu 矢田部老 (?–764) who was able to retrieve the bell and seal again, but was then killed. Eventually the bell and seal fell into Kōken's hands.[57]

Following this struggle, Nakamaro fled to Ōmi.[58] Historically, this province was closely linked with the Fujiwara, since Fuhito had acted as an official at Awaumi, and Muchimaro had once been appointed governor (*kokushu*) there. Nakamaro seems to have had the feeling that the province was his base and

---

[55] Kimoto, *Fujiwara no Nakamaro: sossei wa satoku kashikoku shite*, 305–306.
[56] The bell (鈴) and seal (*nai'in* 内印) are mentioned in the *Yōrō shokuin ryo* 養老職員令 where it is indicated they were supposed to be kept by the Shōnagon. Matsuo, *Tenpyō no seiji no sōran*, 285. They also appear in the *SN* in the edict of Tenpyō hōji 8 (764).9.20: " Nakamaro...sought to seize the bell and seal (鈴印) and snatch away the imperial rank and give it to Prince Shioyaki." Adapted from Bender, *The Edicts of the Last Empress, 749–770*, 86.
[57] Matsuo, *Tenpyō no seiji to sōran*, 286. *SN*, Tenpyō hōji 8 (764).9.11. See also Nakanishi, *Shoku nihongi to nara ōchō no seihen*, 211.
[58] Matsuo, *Tenpyō no seiji to sōran* , 287.

his best opportunity to quickly raise soldiers against Kōken, but his intentions were foreseen and the Seta bridge over the river Uji was destroyed, cutting Nakamaro off from Ōmi. He then moved towards Arachi no Seki in Echizen to try and join his son Shikachi 藤原辛加知 (?–764).[59] It is not certain whether or not Junnin was effectively put under house arrest but with the monarch being in the capital and Nakamaro in Echizen without the seal, it was not difficult for Kōken to portray him as an enemy of the court. In an attempt to solve the matter, Nakamaro thereupon 'enthroned' one of Tenmu's grandsons, Prince Shioyaki 塩焼王 (?–764), and attempted to create a new court in Ōmi.[60]

His move north to join his son was blocked by Mononobe no Hironari 物部広成 (?–?), who supported Kōken. Shikachi was captured and Nakamaro found himself without support and trapped. Following a short but heavy battle, all were captured and put to death by Iware no Iwatate 石村石楯 (?–?).[61] Following the execution of Nakamaro, Retired Sovereign Kōken issued an edict on Tenpyō Hōji 8 (764).9.20, which paints the former Daishi Nakamaro in no uncertain terms: "The Memorials he offered up previously were all lies and flattery. Now we understand that he wished to seize all the throne's power for himself…"[62] In the aftermath of the rebellion, the Retired Sovereign then moved to dispatching troops to Junnin's mansion, stripping him from his rank as sovereign and 'banished' him to Awaji as a court official. Once again, her words left no room for doubt, invoking former sovereign Shōmu's words in proclaiming that Junnin was not only unfit to rule but, in addition, had conspired with Nakamaro against the line of sovereigns.[63]

---

[59] The bridge was destroyed by Hisakabe no Komaro 日下部 子麻呂 (?–773), Nakanishi, *Shoku nihongi to nara ōchō no seihen*, 213.
[60] *SN* Tenpyō hōji 8 (764).9.18.
[61] Matsuo, *Tenpyō no seiji to sōran*, 294. Iwatate was of low rank, but likely as a result of Nakamaro's execution rose to be a mid-level official. Lowe, *Ritualized Writing: Buddhist Practice and Scriptural Cultures in Ancient Japan*, 70.
[62] Bender, *The Edicts*, 86.
[63] Bender, *The Edicts*, 86.

Many questions remain regarding 'Nakamaro's rebellion' of 764. First of all we should note that the only account of the events are in *Shoki Nihongi*, an official history created by the victors of the war. Second, keeping in mind the subjectivity of the account in the official history, it is not entirely clear who rebelled against whom. Later generations have accepted the narrative that Nakamaro was the one to rise against the sovereign, but is this interpretation of the events correct? One might also argue that Nakamaro was serving Junnin, and that it was the Retired Sovereign (Kōken) who rose against the legitimate sovereign. In addition, Matsuo notes the speed with which Nakamaro's flight was countered: would it have been possible for Kibi no Makibi and others to act that fast if Nakamaro was the one who unexpectedly staged a revolt? The conflict between Nakamaro and Kōken had been long in the making. On the one hand, Nakamaro militarized his power, while Kōken on the other did not remain inactive. It is clear that she prepared alliances and kept a close eye on Nakamaro's actions.[64]

□

Nakamaro's religious policies

One of the common misconceptions about Nakamaro is that he was almost exclusively interested in Confucian thought, but he had a larger interest in the culture of Tang China, and there are indications that he attached great value to Buddhism. He constructed temples, sponsored statues, the copying of texts, and borrowed texts from Tōdaiji. On Nakamaro's estate in Tamura, for example, a private scriptorium produced commentaries and treatises, while another one at his son's residence was involved in the copying of sutras.[65] These private projects may have been sanctioned by

---

[64] Matsuo, *Tenpyō no seiji to sōran*, 295. Nakanishi also points out that the account in *Shoku Nihongi* was carefully constructed to portray Nakamaro as the aggressor. Nakanishi, *Shoku Nihongi to nara chō no seihen*, 224–225.
[65] Lowe, *Ritualized Writing*, 140.

Kōmyō but nevertheless took place through Nakamaro's own initiative and personal resources. Two aspects of Nakamaro's religious policies deserve brief mention. First, his role in the copying of the *Heart Sutra* (Skt.:*Prajñāpāramitāhṛdaya sūtra*; Jpn.: *Hannya shingyō* 般若心経) in 757 and, second, his active sponsorship of the Vimalakīrti Assembly through an edict of the same year.

The documents in the Shōsoin repository include several examples of the *Heart Sutra*, but one dating from 758 mentions that it was commissioned by the *Shibi naishō*, the title that had been given to Nakamaro in 757.[66] In addition, in 763 Nakamaro seems to have ordered a thousand copies of the sutra (*shingyō issen kan* 心経一千巻), a project that may never have been completed.[67] There might have been several reasons for Nakamaro's preference for this particular Buddhist text. First, it should be noted that he was influenced by the monk Chikō from Gangōji and therefore treated this text as a state-protecting sutra. Second, both instances of 757 and 763 connect the production of this text with specific political circumstances. It is argued that the version of 757 was aimed at subduing an 'anti-Nakamaro' faction, while the other from 763 falls right in the middle of Nakamaro's growing conflict with Kōken. By this time, the copying of sutras was carried out at the Tōdaiji Construction Agency and was controlled by Kōken and Dōkyō.[68] It is possible that Nakamaro's order was connected to an attempt at taking back control.

□

[66] Miyazaki Kenji, *Nihon kodai no shakyō to shakai*, 160–161; Kimoto, *Fujiwara no Nakamaro*, 91; Bender, *The Edicts*, 71. Lowe refers to this manuscript in the context of household scriptoria. In this case, Nakamaro's copying of this sutra probably should be interpreted as a part of his effort to regain power after Tachibana no Naramaro's revolt the year before. Lowe, *Ritualized Writing*, 91.

[67] Miyazaki points out that this copying project is only mentioned in one document issued by the Tōdaji Construction Agency, dated Tenpyō hōji 7 (763).12.25. Miyazaki Kenji, *Nihon kodai no shakyō to shakai*, 189–190.

[68] Miyazaki, *Nihon kodai no shakyō to shakai*, 189–193.

Nakamaro and Tōshi Kaden

Although there is no document that proves Nakamaro authored or commissioned *Tōshi Kaden*, the beginning of the Chronicle of Kamatari identifies its author as the 'Great Master' (*Taishi*, 大師), a title that was conferred on Nakamaro by Retired Sovereign Kōken in 760.[69] Most Japanese scholars, Okimori, Hasebe, Shinokawa among them, accepted him as either the author or the sponsor of the chronicles.[70] It is worth stressing that these biographies serve to confirm not just the legitimacy of the Fujiwara, but Nakamaro's own political position. The narratives can be seen as the product of 'genealogical interests' in which Nakamaro sought to establish the authority of his line.[71] Not long after the death of the main four Fujiwara brothers in the epidemic of 737, the position of the Fujiwara at court was precarious and even in the late 750s Nakamaro's authority was still fragile. Second, in the description of the lives of Nakamaro's ancestors, the unbreakable bond between sovereign and servant is emphasized. To legitimize this relation, very often concepts and phrases from Chinese origin are used, such as references to the Book of Rites, the *History of the Han*, the *Huainanzi* or the *Spring and Autumn Annals*. It should be noted that some of these quotes made their way to the History through the *Nihon Shoki*, while other parts were quoted directly from these sources. This shows that the *Tōshi Kaden* borrows from the *Nihon Shoki*, but also adds information and constructs its own narrative, different from the imperial histories.

The significance of *Tōshi Kaden* is made clear in the beginning of the first part, the Chronicle of Kamatari. Here, the origins of the Nakatomi are explained in sacred terms, referring to gods mentioned in *Kojiki*. We are told that Nakatomi no Kamatari was

---

[69] Bender, *The Edicts*, 84. Kishi, *Fujiwara no Nakamaro*, 293.

[70] *TK*, 121. Okimori points out that both '大師' and '太師' are used; Hasebe mentioned that the *Kaden* was composed during Nakamaro's rule and points at the importance of the Chronicle of Muchimaro being authored by the monk Enkei. Hasebe, "Fujiwara no Nakamoro," 180–181. Shinokawa includes several essays on Nakamaro's influence on the content and style of the *Tōshi Kaden*.

[71] I borrow the expression 'genealogical interests' from Torquil Duthie in his analysis of the *Nihon Shoki*. Duthie, *The Jinshin Rebellion*, 316.

in fact a descendant of the divine *Ame no Koyane no Mikoto*, and that his clan mediated between the gods and men, hence the name 'Nakatomi' (中臣). This mediation between heaven and earth is well exemplified by the role played by the Nakatomi in the *Ritual of Great Purification* (*Ōharae* 大祓). The prayers of this ritual included in the early ninth century *Engi shiki* 延喜式 describe how the Nakatomi were central in establishing a relation between the terrestrial and heavenly *kami*, bridging the world of men with the heavenly realm:

> ...let the Ōnakatomi take the sacred branches...lay them upon the many offering tables...and recite the solemn liturgy of the heavenly magic formula...may the heavenly *kami* push open the worthy doors of Heaven....may the terrestrial *kami* ascend to the summits of the high mountains...[72]

In the story of Amaterasu and Susano-o, the *Kojiki* mentions that the gods *Ame no Koyane no Mikoto* and *Futa Tama no Mikoto* 'brought out the mirror and showed it to the goddess *Amaterasu-o-mi-kami*.'[73] The opening phrase thus links Kamatari's ancestral deity with the divine imperial one, originating in Amaterasu. In other words, from ancient times the Nakatomi/Fujiwara are inseparable from the line of sovereigns. The *Tōshi Kaden* cultivates this bond by celebrating the Fujiwara clan as the sovereign's highest servants.

The study of the *Tōshi Kaden* is important to understand the political and factional developments from the seventh through the eighth century mainly for two reasons. First, the text is clearly a composite of quotes and paraphrases of older Chinese and Japanese sources, revealing important clues regarding the representation

---

[72] Hardacre, *Shinto*, 116–118. Bock, *Engi-Shiki* 2, 86. Both male and female members of the Nakatomi were involved in these rites. For a good example of the role of Nakatomi women in court rites, see Bock, *Engi-Shiki* 1, 84–85.

[73] Ebersole, *Ritual Poetry and the Politics of Death in Early Japan*, 97. The *sonpi bunmyaku* identifies Kamatari's father as 'Mikeko'. He is called the 'Great Ancestor of the Fujiwara' (藤原大祖是也) and identified as a son of Katanosa no Ōmuraji 可多能古大連 (?–?), a 17th generation descendant of the divine *Ame no Koyane no Mikoto*.

of sovereignty and the authority of the court. Second, the source does not just reveal us information about the origins of the Fujiwara but, more importantly, seems to describe Nakamaro's view on his political situation and time but expressed through the events of the previous century. In other words, when learning about Kamatari's actions and decisions in relation to the position of the sovereign, we should imagine that we are in fact looking at Nakamaro himself and the challenges he faced. In addition to looking at the actual content of the text, it is equally important to take note of what is missing. Later texts such as the Origin Chronicles of Kōfukuji (*Kōfukuji engi* 興福寺縁起) describe Kamatari and his wife as the founders of both Kōfukuji's predecessor *Yamashinadera* (山階寺) and its main ritual, the Yuima-e.[74] However, in the *Tōshi Kaden* the temple is only mentioned in passing, which seems peculiar given Kōfukuji's status as Fujiwara clan temple and its expansion around the middle of the Nara period. Provided that Nakamaro needed to provide legitimacy to his line, the absence of this narrative is peculiar. In addition, an edict issued in 757 regarding the donation of tax land to the Yuima-e does not mention Kamatari's illness either.[75] Why did Nakamaro omit this part? This is especially intriguing since in the centuries to follow, Kōfukuji, the adjacent Kasuga shrine, and the Yuima-e would be identified with the power and lustre of the Northern Fujiwara.

□

Scholarship on Tōshi Kaden

In recent years Japanese scholars have shown an increasing interest in Nakamaro and *Tōshi Kaden*. One of the earliest works is Kishi's general study, which still serves as one of the best introductions to Nakamaro, although it remains essentially descriptive.

---

[74] KE, 320. The text describes how Kamatari's wife, Kagami no Ōkimi asks him for permission three times before she is allowed to construct a site of worship.
[75] For the edict see Togashi, *Fujiwara no Nakamaro ni okeru yuima-e*, 101.

A few decades later, in 2011, Kimoto published *Fujiwara no Nakamaro*, which approaches Nakamaro from various points of view: literary studies, religion, and institutional history. In 2013, the same author edited *Fujiwara no Nakamaro seiken to sono jidai* (*The Political Power of Nakamaro and his Times*) in which fifteen scholars addressed Nakamaro's importance for the reception of Tang culture, the development of the legal system, and the production of poetry among much else. What renders this study of utmost importance for the student of the eighth century, is that it connects literary, religious and institutional developments, and by doing so connects his institutional changes, such as his implementation of *ritsuryō* laws promulgated by Fuhito, to the reception of Chinese histories, sponsorship of Buddhist rituals, and the composition of poetry. It also discusses the relation between the Fujiwara and other factions at court, re-evaluating the image of Nakamaro as 'usurper', and allowing us to reflect on his institutional and intellectual influence.[76]

Tōshi kaden wo yomu (*Reading Tōshi Kaden*), edited by Shinokawa and Masuo, provides an in-depth historical and literary analysis of the work itself, and several decades after Hiraoka first published an annotated version of the Chronicle of Kamatari, Okimori edited the first complete annotated version of all three chronicles in his *Tōshi kaden, Kamatari, Jōe, Muchimaro den, chū shaku to kenkyū*, incorporating various extant manuscripts from the Kamakura to the Edo periods. In the West, Bender, Ooms and Piggott have mentioned Nakamaro's importance, but there is as yet no work that focuses on his life and work. There is, however, one exception. The German missionary Hermann Bohner, a prolific translator who worked on many sources such as the *Nihon Ryōiki* and several works on Regent Shōtoku Taishi 聖徳太子 (574–622), wrote "Kamatari-den, Taishoku kwanden Kaden, d.i. Haustraditionen des Hauses Fujiwara" (1941) and "Muchimaro-den. Kaden, d.i. Haustraditionen des Hauses Fujiwara" (1942).

---

[76] Kimoto also points out that in the prewar period research on the Nara period, Nakamaro was certainly seen as someone who acted against the imperial system. After WWII, however, this bias seems to have gradually disappeared. Kimoto, *Fujiwara no Nakamaro seiken to sono jidai*, 1–2.

These German translations are reliable, although from time to time they betraying signs of the nationalism of the times.[77] In 2002, John Bentley included a translation of the *Chronicle of Kamatari* in his study on early Japanese historiography, but it should be noted that the present translation differs considerably, partly because a different source text has been chosen.

The present translation is based on the critical edition by Okimori, Satō and Yajima. As explained by the editors, this edition is based on two manuscripts, although these versions are constantly compared with the remainder of older manuscripts of the *Tōshi Kaden*. The 'upper part' or the Chronicle of Kamatari is based on the manuscript *Taishōkan kamatari kō kaden* 大織冠鎌足公家伝 included in the *Kyū fushimi miyake zō* 旧伏見宮家蔵. The 'lower part' of the *Tōshi Kaden*, namely the chronicles of Jōe and Muchimaro, are based on the manuscript from the eighteenth century owned by the National Diet Library.[78] As pointed out by Okimori, several pre-modern sources such as the Heian period *Fusō ryakki* 扶桑略記 or the twelfth century *Tōdaiji yōroku* 東大寺要録 do contain several excerpts from the eighth-century *Tōshi Kaden* and the editors of the critical edition have taken these other sources into account in their publication.[79] The translation below is primarily based on Okimura's text, but where necessary comparisons have been made with the text as published in the *Nihon shisō taikei* and the *Gunshō ruijū*.

---

[77] Bohner, "Kamatari-Den. Taishokukwan-den. Kaden, d.i. Haustraditionen (des Hauses Fujiwara) Oberer (Band)," 207–245; Bohner, "Muchimaro-Den: Kaden, d.i. Haustraditionen (des Hauses Fujiwara) Unterer (Band)," 412–436.
[78] Okimori, *Tōshi kaden*, 9.
[79] Okimori, *Tōshi kaden*, 12.

Part II

Narratives of the three extant chronicles[1]

⌘

The Chronicle of Kamatari

THE FIRST SECTION of *Tōshi Kaden* describes the life of the patriarch of the Fujiwara line, Nakatomi no Kamatari, the eldest son of Nakatomi no Mikeko 中臣美気祜 (?–?), information which is also confirmed in *Kugyō bunin*.[2] In the context of Sovereign Jomei's 舒明天皇 (593–641) reign, the *Nihon Shoki* refers to Kamatari's father as *Nakatomi no Muraji Mike* 中臣連彌氣, and mentions that he was one of four officials.[3] Virtually nothing is known about his father but it is suggested that he was instrumental in the instalment of Jomei.[4] On the death of Jomei in 641, Kamatari witnessed the dispute regarding his succession, a conflict that resulted in the dismissal and eventual forced suicide of Crown Prince Yamashiro no Ōe 山背大兄王 (?–643), the son of the illustrious Shōtoku Taishi, and the enthronement of Jomei's consort Kōgyoku.[5]

Tōshi Kaden starts exactly at this moment. Having elaborated on Kamatari's intellectual talents and his sense of morality,

---

[1] Below, the designation History refers to the whole of the three texts, whereas 'chronicle' refers to one its three parts; the chronicle of Kamatari, Jōe or Muchimaro.
[2] See also *Nakatomi uji keizu* in *SB*, 194.
[3] *NS*, 218. As mentioned by Okimura, his name is written as Mikeko 御食子 in the *Nakatomi uji keizu* 中臣氏系図, *TK*, 117. *GR* 5, 191 and 194.
[4] Inoue, "The Century of Reform", 191.
[5] Yamashiro was attacked by Iruka's forces and committed suicide with his family, marking the end of Shōtoku Taishi's lineage.

the chronicle narrates that the courtier Soga no Kuratsukuri 蘇我鞍作 (?–645), more commonly referred to as Iruka 入鹿 'increased his own fortune' and controlled the court.

Iruka was the son of Soga no Emishi 蘇我蝦夷 (?–645), the head of the Soga, who was responsible for the removal of Prince Yamashiro and Jomei's enthronement. After having gained ground at court, he was quick to move against Prince Yamashiro, and during the ensuing standoff led by his son Iruka, the prince and twenty-three other descendants of Shōtoku's line perished. Due to the bloody repression of this part of the imperial family in 642 and his autocratic behaviour at court, discontent grew, and it is here that Kamatari started to play a significant role. The Chronicle of Kamatari details how the Fujiwara patriarch very gradually and in great secrecy started a plot that involved Prince Naka no Ōe, the later sovereign Tenji, and a member of the Soga clan, Soga no Ishikawa no Maro 蘇我石川麻呂 (?–649), whose family had supported Prince Yamashiro. The text describes how the high-minded servant Kamatari convinced his later sovereign Naka no Ōe to follow the will of the people and have his uncle Prince Karu enthroned.

The Chronicle of Kamatari's version of the events on the 12th day of the 6th month of 645 is derived from, and sometimes borrowed from, *Nihon Shoki*. The text describes how Iruka was killed during a declaration of a memorial from the Three Kingdoms by the official Yamada no Omi. After the assassination, Kōgyoku abdicated and Prince Karu became sovereign as Kōtoku 孝徳天皇 (596–654). In the aftermath of this revolt and the enthronement of the new sovereign, now Crown Prince Naka no Ōe assumed a leading role over state affairs, while Abe no Uchi Maro no Omi became Minister of the Left, Soga no Ishikawa no Maro Minister of the Right and Kamatari himself was promoted to Middle Counsellor, remaining at the sovereign and the crown prince's side.

The chronicle starts with a short description of the Nakatomi's significance, quickly moves on to Kamatari's mother's auspicious pregnancy, describing how the length of pregnancy was unusual and his voice could be heard while still in the womb. Moving on to his childhood and youth, the text then provides an account of the young Kamatari's intelligence, personality and interests. The text then delves into the turbulent 640s and describes in more detail Kamatari's relation to Prince Naka no Ōe, describing the slow evolution towards the murder of Soga no Iruka and the ensuing Taika reforms. Finally, we learn that the country and its people were put at ease under the benevolent rule of Tenji and Kamatari. While this might seem simplistic at first sight, a close reading of the text, and a comparison between the time it was written and the events it refers to shows a complex composite history that provides us deeper insight into the alleged author Nakamaro's use of history and the ways in which he viewed the role of the Fujiwara. In other words, while reading the Chronicle of Kamatari, and the subsequent chronicles, the reader has to keep in mind that the text was composed in the second half of the eighth century to confirm the connection between the Fujiwara and the line of sovereigns. Two themes seem to be crucial in the Chronicle of Kamatari: first, the Fujiwara patriarch as the sovereign's main, moral servant and, second, the Fujiwara's ability to be in close proximity to the sovereign. Both aspects are not limited to Kamatari's biography and are carried over in the following two biographies of the patriarch's descendants.

From the very beginning, Kamatari's character and high morality are emphasized, character traits that allow him to serve as the sovereign's main servant and advisor. But how should we understand 'servant' in his case? Kamatari is not a blind follower. Through references to Chinese histories and past examples of great moral behaviour, the chronicle paints Kamatari as the ideal servant/minister who guides, and at times even reprimands, the sovereign for the greater good of the state. The moral dilemma that runs throughout the first part of the Chronicle of Kamatari, concerns the decision to murder Soga no Iruka. In a question-and-answer format, we find Prince Naka no Ōe caught between protecting the state on the one hand, while not damaging the relation between servant and ruler on the other. The narrative can be summarized as follows.

First, it is made clear that Kamatari is an exceptional man and loyal servant to Tenji. Second, it is pointed out that he is knowledgeable in the Confucian classics. Third, he overthrows the Soga after murdering Iruka. Finally, he is able to restore the power of the sovereign after the destruction of the usurpers, the Soga.⁶

Terms used in this narrative and which resonate with a variety of Chinese histories and the Confucian classics include *daiji* (大事; 'great matters'), *yūryaku* (雄略; 'ingenuity') and to a lesser extent *tengyō* (天業) and *daigyō* (大業), both referring to great abilities to direct the matters of state.

The following passage illustrates the meaning of 'great matter'. After the abduction scene of Prince Yamada's daughter we read:

太臣諫曰既定天下之大事何忿家中之小過。
中之大兄即止矣。⁷

> The Great Minister admonished him: 'A great matter under Heaven has been settled, why be angry about a small matter that occurred in your house?' Naka no Ōe immediately stopped.

Naka no Ōe decides to accept Kamatari's advice and the matter is settled. The word 'great matter' (*daiji*) occurs earlier on in the text as well, when Kamatari and Naka no Ōe first meet. Prior to their first encounter, Kamatari stated the following about Prince Karu:

皇子器量不足与謀大事

> … the prince's abilities were insufficient for planning such a great matter.⁸

In other words, he is not suitable to join a rebellion and save the state. The text then immediately draws a comparison with Naka no Ōe and stresses that, in contrast, the future sovereign Tenji does indeed possess the necessary 'ingenuity' or *yūryaku*:

---

⁶ Go, "Nihon shoki to shunju kuyōden", 3.
⁷ *TK*, 75.
⁸ *TK*, 154.

更欲択君歴見王宗唯中大兄雄略英徹可与撥乱[9]

If the Great Minister wanted to select someone, going through the entire royal family, then only Naka no Ōe was ingenious, heroic and able to eliminate disorder.[10]

This suggests that ingenuity is seen to be a necessary condition to accomplish the 'great matters of state' and it is apparent that of all the members of the court it is only Tenji and Kamatari who possess this quality. Both men are seen to complement each other. It is Kamatari who is able to recognize the trait of ingenuity in the later sovereign and thus 'decides' who the future monarch should be. In other words, Naka no Ōe will become the monarch Tenji but the one who has the genius to recognize this is Kamatari. The Fujiwara and the line of sovereigns are inseparable and rely on one another. At the end this is illustrated when Tenji follows Kamatari's funeral procession weeping. "With whom shall we direct the country, with whom shall we govern the people? Each time I reflect upon this, my sadness cuts even deeper," he cries.[11]

□

The Chronicle of Jōe

THE SECOND SECTION of *Tōshi Kaden* contains a short description and eulogy of the life of one of Japan's earliest monks, Kamatari's eldest son Jōe (643–665; 貞慧). Although this biography is attributed to Enkei (延慶; ?–?), a monk close to Nakamaro who is also accredited with the third chronicle, its authorship in fact remains unclear.[12] The relation between the Kamatari and Jōe biographies is not self-evident. Joe's chronicle differs in that there is no borrowing of passages from *Nihon Shoki*, a point highlighted

---

[9] *TK*, 141.
[10] 'Ingenious' refers to the term *yūryaku* (雄略), a word that also appears in the *Nihon Shoki*. See below under the Chronicle of Kamatari for a detailed explanation and references to Chinese sources.
[11] *TK*, 245.
[12] *TK*, 291.

by Kishi.¹³ Jōe is mentioned in *Nihon Shoki* as part of an envoy to Tang China, and his passing is likewise mentioned, but it is remarkable that there are no larger parallels. This raises the possibility that Jōe's text was never meant to be aligned with Kamatari's. Research by several Japanese specialists has, however, suggested that this is not the case and that Jōe's biography was meant to link to Kamatari's from the very outset. There are three reasons why this may be the case. First, at the end of the Chronicle of Kamatari, the existence of both Fuhito and Jōe's biographies is mentioned. Second, the eulogy included in Jōe's biography is in fact directed towards Kamatari. It is clear that this part of the text wants to demonstrate that the virtues of Kamatari carried over to his offspring, and in extension to other Fujiwara descendants. By reading the celebration of Jōe's life, we are urged to remember the greatness of the patriarch, and in extension perhaps the text's patron, Nakamaro. In this sense, the Chronicle of Jōe can be seen as a logical extension of Kamatari's biography. Third, Endō and Okimori demonstrate that the usage of certain expressions suggest that the narratives were meant to be linked .¹⁴

Apart from these three elements, it is also useful to look at both biographies from the point of view of the connection between Kamatari and the emerging Buddhist tradition. We know that Kamatari was connected to the foundation of Yamashinadera (which became Kōfukuji) and the start of one of pre-modern Japan's most important rituals, the Vimalakīrti Assembly. The tenth century *Kōfukuji engi* written by Fujiwara no Yoshiyo 藤原良世 (823–900) provides the following account not found in *Tōshi Kaden*:

> The Prime Minster Fujiwara no Kamatari humbly spoke a Great Vow dedicated to the Peace and Quiet of the Imperial House and the Eternity of the State and started this assembly (the Yuima-e) for the first time. Soon afterwards, the Prime Minster was overcome by illness. In order for him to recover, a meditation nun from Paekche named Pŏmmyŏng (Jap.: Hōmyō; 法明) told the Prime Minister: ' I practice the Great Vehicle and there is a Sūtra called the Vimalakīrti in which a chapter on

---

[13] Kishi, *Fujiwara no nakamaro*, 299–300.
[14] Fujii, "Fujiwara Nakamaro to nittōsō Jōe", 217–218.

illness is included. I will read and recite it for you and maybe you will recover from your illness.' Before she had even finished one chapter, the illness of the Prime Minster settled. At that time, the Prime Minister bowed his head, folded his hands and spoke: 'Continuous life cycles return in accordance with the teachings of the Great Vehicle. The meditation nun will become lecturer and lecture on the Vimalakīrti Sūtra incessantly for a period of three days.' In the period after Fujiwara no Kamatari, the ritual was discontinued. This was in Keiun 2 (705), the year of the Wood Snake, in the seventh month of autumn.[15]

We find a similar account in the tenth century *Sanbō'e kotoba* 三宝絵詞 by Minamoto no Tamenori 源爲憲 (?–1011), though this adds further details:

> In the past, the Great Minister of the Interior Kamatari lived at a mansion in Suehara located in Yamashina near Uji. He fell very ill and did not recover. At that time there was a nun from Silla present at his house and she asked the Great Minister of the Interior: " Are there in this country people who suffer from illness?" He responded : "There are." Then he asked " Can you cure them? " She responded : " Construct an image of the layman Vimalakīrti. If you read the *Vimalakīrti Sūtra*, the illness will cease." Thereupon, the Great Minister built a hall at his mansion and constructed an image there. He had the sūtra read and the nun was made Lecturer. On the first day, she lectured on the chapter on illness. The sickness of the Great Minister thereupon vanished. From the following year this event took place yearly. When the Great Minister passed away, his second son Fuhito was still young. Gradually he made career and he also was promoted to the position of Great Minister. [Just like his father] he fell ill, caused by the interruption of the Vimalakīrti Assembly. For this reason, Fuhito revived the Vimalakīrti Assembly and moved it from the mansion at Suehara to the Hokke temple. From the Hokke temple it was moved to Uetsukidera. Afterwards, Great Minister Fuhito built Kōfukuji. Because he moved the hall from his Suehara mansion in Yamashina to the new capital in Nara, he called it Yamashina Temple[16]

---

[15] KE, 321–322. Also cited by Takayama, 63.
[16] Own translation. *Sanbō'e kotoba*, *DNBZ* 111, 102. The term used for 'lecturer' in this text is *kōshi* 講師.

The account related to Kamatari's founding of the temple at Yamashina and his involvement with the start of the Vimalakīrti Assembly can be found in several other sources. For example, the oldest source related to the origins of Kōfukuji, *Kyūki* 旧記, provides the following order of events.[17] First, after the Taika palace revolt of 645, the point where the Chronicle of Kamatari begins, the Great Minister erects a statue of the historical Buddha, possibly an entire triad to which Four Heavenly Kings were added. Second, Kamatari falls ill and his wife Kagami no Ōkimi builds a temple at Yamashina, the site of their residence. Third, this temple is then moved to Umayasaka, and referred to as Umayasakadera. Fourth, this building is moved and reconstructed in the new capital, Heijōkyō, marking the beginning of Kōfukuji's large monastic complex.[18] This elaborate story of one of pre-modern Japan's largest monasteries cannot be found in the Chronicle of Kamatari, perhaps because it fulfilled a different purpose. The founding of a clan temple might not have been relevant in a narrative that describes the unbreakable bond between servant and monarch. Jōe's biography, on the other hand, certainly does introduce Buddhism as a topic. One can only speculate why a monk's biography would be inserted at this point, but it is possible that a connection had to be created between Kamatari and the monastic community. Kōfukuji would eventually become the head temple of the Hossō school ('Dharma characteristics'; 法相) and de facto functioned as the Fujiwara's clan temple alongside the family's main shrine on the fields of Kasuga. Nothing is known about Jōe's monastic training and at this early stage of Japanese Buddhism one could not necessarily assume he was a Hossō monk. However, as pointed out by Itō, the Chronicle of Jōe might have been included to demonstrate Kamatari's personal relation to the emerging Buddhist tradition. The Chronicle of Kamatari describes the patriarch's life but after the episode of his passing returns to his faith in Buddhism and even briefly mentions the Vimalakīrti Assembly. The text states:

---

[17] *KR*, 6.

[18] Miyai, *Ritsuryō kizoku fujiwara-shi no ujigami ujidera shinkō to sobyō-saishi*, 161.

It was the Great Minister's character to honour the Three Jewels. He revered them and spread them in the four directions. Each year in the tenth month, he erected a platform to expound the Dharma, to revere the Great Way of the Vimalakīrti Sūtra, and expound the marvelous principle of non-duality. In addition, the possessions of his household were divided and deposed at Gangōji, to enhance the study of the Five Teachings. Thus the lineage of eminent priests was not cut off and the Way of the Holy One prospered.[19]

Here, the text does mention Kamatari's belief, an aspect of his personality not stated in the *Nihon Shoki*. It is very well possible, of course, that this is a later embellishment, added under Nakamaro.[20] If it was added by Nakamaro, then the chronicles of Kamatari and the monk Jōe become part of Nakamaro's power struggle in which he had to justify the authority of his line and strengthen the connection between him and the growing Kōfukuji. In this sense, both chronicles also appear closely connected.

Although not much is known about Jōe, he is usually mentioned because of his suspicious death. Apart from this biography and several passages in *Nihon Shoki*, he is also mentioned in the later *Tō nomine ryakki* (多武峯略記) and in the *Genkō shakusho* (元亨釈書). *Nihon Shoki* mentions that in 653, the young Jōe was among one hundred and twenty people who travelled to Chang'an. Part of the same envoy was also the well-known monk Dōshō 道昭 (629–700). A later entry from the same source states he returned to the Japanese court in 665 where he unexpectedly passed away.[21]

It is interesting to note that Jōe is mentioned as Kamatari's eldest son, while his younger brother Fuhito would become one of the most important Fujiwara officials of the eighth century. The image of Kamatari as patriarch, flanked by his two sons Jōe and Fuhito, in monastic and courtly attire respectively, symbolizes the role the Fujiwara had assumed as the court's main bureaucratic and monastic line. However, uncertainty still exists

---

[19] *TK*, 253.
[20] Fujii, "Fujiwara nakamaro to nyūtō zō Jōe", 222.
[21] Bingenheimer, *A Biographical Dictionary*, 41; Fujii, "Fujiwara Nakamaro to nyūtō zō Jōe" 219–220.

regarding Jōe's identity. It is puzzling, for example, that it was the eldest son who became a monk. Later sources suggest an alternative version. *Genkō shakusho* describes Jōe as Kamatari's adopted son, rather than as his biological descendant. This text states that Kōtoku Tennō and one of his consorts were Jōe's actual parents. Upon his birth, the child was given to Kamatari, who had the boy study under the Korean monk Hye'un 慧隱.[22] On the hand this may explain why it was Fuhito who became the official and why Jōe became a monk, but on the other it also stresses the bond between both brothers. The text explains how Jōe dreamed about his father's demise and upon his return consulted with Fuhito on Kamatari's passing. As a result of their meeting, they decide to move their father's remains and give him a second burial, an event narrated with strong Buddhist overtones.[23]

Much uncertainty also remains regarding the exact circumstances of Jōe's death. His chronicle suggests that he died shortly after his return to the Japanese court and that he may have been poisoned by officials from Paekche, something that is also found in *Nihon Shoki*.

□

The Chronicle of Muchimaro

At the end of the Chronicle of Kamatari, it is mentioned that both Jōe and Fuhito's biography were also included. Unfortunately, the latter is no longer extant, if it was ever written. It is possible that parts of the original *Fuhito den* 不比等伝 were included in the eighth century *Kyūki*, but there does not seem to be any scholarly consensus as regards this claim.[24]

The third and final part of *Tōshi Kaden* concerns Fuhito's son, Kamatari's grandson, Fujiwara no Muchimaro. Although the text

---

[22] Bingenheimer, *A Biographical Dictionary*, 117. Bingenheimer refers to him as 'Eun'.
[23] Bingenheimer, *A Biographical Dictionary*, 118.
[24] Fukuyama, *Nihon kenchiku shi kenkyū*, 332.

celebrates his life and gives him literary and governmental talent, he never was able to reach high status. This may have been related to poor health, but it should also be remembered that he died early during the infamous smallpox epidemic of 737. His biography paints a heroic, almost superhuman, image. He is knowledgeable about Daoist matters, excels at the Confucian classics, has an important role in the education of Fujiwara officials at the court's academy (*daigaku* 大学), and is mentioned in the context of what may be the earliest reference to the Shinto-Buddhist phenomenon of *honji suijaku* (本地垂迹), a theory in which native deities were considered manifestations of Buddhist divinities.[25] His experiences are also explicitly compared to those of Yamato Takeru, an early mythical hero included in the *Kojiki*.

As is the case in Kamatari's biography, Muchimaro is described in terms adapted from the Chinese Classics. From the outset his virtue and knowledge are celebrated, both necessary prerequisites to become an upright servant to the sovereign. Describing his youth, the text reads:

> As years went by, he [Muchimaro] did not associate himself with trivial matters....What was not respectful, he did not adopt; what was not righteous, he did not request.[26]

The term 'trivial matter' (小節) appears in several Chinese sources such as the *Shiji* and refers to those occupations that do not contribute to the development of the virtues of righteousness (義) and principle (理). The second part of the statement is paraphrased from the *Yijing*. All this suggests that his character was out of the ordinary and reminiscent of his grandfather, Kamatari, although Muchimaro's intellectual side is stressed over his career. Two episodes from Muchimaro's biography warrant a closer reading, both related to events of an overt religious nature: the encounter with a *kami*, and the comparison between Muchimaro and the mythical Yamato Takeru.

---

[25] Ooms, *Imperial Politics and Symbolics in Ancient Japan*, 194. *Honji suijaku* can be translated as "original forms of deities and their local traces", Teeuwen and Rambelli, *Buddhas and Kami in Japan*, 1.
[26] *TK*, 296.

The eighth century saw the emergence of 'shrine temples' or *jingūji* 神宮寺, in principle combinatory sites where Buddhist temples were built next to shrines dedicated to *kami*.²⁷ Stories regarding the foundation of these shrine temples can be found in many Origin Chronicles (*engi*) and the Chronicle of Muchimaro contains the earliest mention of such a combinatory shrine temple. The story is as follows [abridged]²⁸:

> In the past, the minister [Muchimaro] met a strange man in a dream. His looks were unusual and he said: 'Men and gods know you adore and yearn for the law of the Buddha. Please construct a temple for me, and help me to fulfill my vow. Because of past karma, I became a deity long ago…'²⁹

The story continues with Muchimaro reflecting on the relation between *kami* and men and finally building a site of worship: "The ways of men and gods are different…the hidden and apparent are not the same…He built a temple, known as a *jingūji* in Koshinomichi. " I suggest three elements are of importance in this narrative. First, the founding of this particular shrine-complex, Kehi in Echizen, was undertaken by a senior Fujiwara official. As Muchimaro was Nakamaro's father, this could mean that Muchimaro is here given the status of main Fujiwara official who had the authority to do so, a position and ability thus implicitly inherited by Nakamaro. Second, the local *kami* described in the story clearly refers to his karmic bonds, presenting a clear example of the *honji suijaku* phenomenon in which 'kami and various Buddhist supernaturals…were ultimately identical.' In other words, a view in which the *kami* were local manifestations of Buddhist figures.³⁰ Interesting to note is that Muchimaro encounters the

---

²⁷ One of the earlier explanations regarding the relation between the Buddha and the kami appears in the *Shoku Nihongi* for the year 766.
²⁸ Also mentioned in Bowring, *Religious Traditions of Japan*, 94. See also Kochinski, *Negotiations between the Kami and Buddha Realms*, 41. Grapard, *The Protocol of the Gods*, 72.
²⁹ *TK*, 351.
³⁰ Hardacre, *Shinto, A History*, 7–8; Tyler, *The Cult of Kasuga seen through its art*, 75. Ooms, *Imperial Politics and Symbolics in Ancient Japan*, 193–195.

kami in a dream, exemplifying how the presence of the *kami* was 'channelled' through Muchimaro, demonstrating he must have been a virtuous and morally pure person: seeing *kami* was not for the ordinary.[31] Third, it is of note that Muchimaro on the one hand founds the temple in his capacity of main Fujiwara official, but on the other also engages in a form of pilgrimage or even mountain asceticism, an image that appears on several occasions in his biography. As pointed out by Teeuwen and Rambelli, such ascetic practice related to the influence of Chinese culture, in which the figure of the wandering saint or ascetic holds a powerful place. In this sense, the image of Muchimaro as ascetic, knowledgeable about both Buddhist and Daoist matters, becomes illustrative of a larger, East Asian literary phenomenon.

While roaming the countryside and probably engaging in ascetic practice, Muchimaro is compared to the mythical Yamato Takeru:

> [Muchimaro said]: I desire to climb mount Ibuki and worship.' The people of the region replied: ' If you enter this mountain, gales, thunder and rain will follow. Clouds and mist will blind all in obscurity, and swarms of wasps will fly up. In the past, Prince Yamato Takeru (*yamato takeru no miko* 倭武皇子) soothed evil demons and spirits of the eastern lands and when he returned to this world, he climbed the mountain…[32]

The biography then adds that Yamato Takeru 'changed into a white bird and flew to the sky'.

According to *Kojiki*, Yamato Takeru was the son of Sovereign Keikō 景行天皇 (?–?) who embodied the bravery of a warrior by defending the emerging Yamato court. Two elements are of great significance here: the identity and ascension of the mountain, and Yamato Takeru's transformation into a white bird.

Kojiki states that Yamato Takeru travels to Mount Ibuki to slay the god of the mountain. However, he fails to recognize that a white boar he encounters in fact is the deity. The god sends down a storm of hail on Yamato Takeru who is injured and finally passes away later on the Nobo plain where his wife and

---

[31] Andreeva, *Assembling Shinto*, 22–23.
[32] *TK*, 340–341.

children construct a tomb for him.³³ Not only is mount Ibuki the site where Yamato Takeru is defeated, it is also a mountain where the hero makes a formal, ritual announcement. Before ascending the mountain, Yamato Takeru proclaims his intention to subdue the wrathful deity. In a same manner, Muchimaro makes a formal declaration before he ascends the same mountain. It is possible that what is evoked here is the ritual of 'gazing over the country' (*kunimi* 国見), a ritual act during which the sovereign or member of the higher nobility confirms sovereignty.³⁴ Muchimaro's fate is however significantly different from Yamato no Takeru's: the latter fails to recognize the deity and perishes, whereas Muchimaro succeeds and survives. Upon death, Yamato Takeru's physical body transforms into the spiritual one of a white bird who flies away to the skies. He does not perish, but merely transforms into a different kind of being. It is not difficult to see a parallel here with the creation of the Fujiwara as a line of servants that transcends common man: just like Yamato Takeru, Muchimaro (and in extension Kamatari), served their sovereign and the court. After having completed their role, their spiritual significance is stressed: just like Yamato Takeru's metamorphosis from a physical into a spiritual form, the Fujiwara themselves are given an elevated, supernatural status. A status only reinforced by the statement in the very beginning of *Tōshi Kaden* that they have divine descent from *Ame no Koyane no Mikoto*.

Kamatari, Jōe and Muchimaro present three radically different personae. First, the patriarch Kamatari is the one who possesses the morality and ingenuity to select the monarch and loyally stay at his side till his death. He is represented as the capable, ideal servant. Second, Jōe is eager and talented, to the extent that jealousy arose, resulting in his murder. His life was cut short at a very young age, but it is suggested he was destined for greatness. Finally, the fascinating picture of Muchimaro presents a wandering sage who seems to embody core Confucian and Daoist principles. He is the ideal *junzi* through correct ritual behaviour, is said to have practiced *wuwei*, and wanders through the country and meets its

---

³³ Levy, *Hitomaro and the Birth of Japanese Lyricism*, 19.
³⁴ Ebersole, *Ritual Poetry*, 23–25.

people, evoking the image of a saint who retreats from society. In addition, when he ascends the mountain and gazes over the realm, reference is made to the mythical Yamato Takeru, elevating Muchimaro himself to an otherworldly status. The three biographies thus represent different personalities but through their differences also consciously contain important continuities. *Tōshi Kaden* can be seen as part of the important endeavour by Nakamaro to restore his line and provide a thorough basis for Fujiwara authority for generations to come. Nakamaro himself perished, but the Fujiwara did survive and prosper. Although it was to be the Northern branch, and not Nakamaro's Southern branch, that prevailed, the Fujiwara remained the most powerful of all court families for centuries to come.

Part III

Translations

⌘

The Chronicle of Kamatari 鎌足伝

UPPER PART OF the House History by the Great Master[1]
Kamatari, the Inner Palace Minister who was also called 'Chūrō,' was a man of the Takechi district of Yamato Province.[2] His forebears descended from Ame no Koyane no Mikoto; for generations they had administered the rites for Heaven and Earth, harmonizing the space between men and the gods.[3] Therefore it was ordered their clan was to be called *Ōnakatomi*.[4]

---

[1] Great Master or *Taishi* (大師); this term refers to Fujiwara no Nakamaro. Bender translated the term as 'Great Preceptor' and points out that this rank is derived from the highest title of the Three Dukes of the Zhou, which clearly shows the influence of continental terminology not only in court bureaucracy but also in the Chronicle. In a decree of 760, Kōken conferred this rank to Nakamaro. This decree stresses Nakamaro's morality (he states he is not worthy receiving it), and draws a clear connection between him and Fuhito, the grandfather of both Nakamaro and the sovereign, Kōken. Bender, *The Edicts*, 83–84.
[2] The meaning of the name Chūrō 仲郎 is not clear. Okimori speculates it points at Nakamaro being his father's second son. *TK*, 118 and 123.
[3] *Ame no Koyane no Mikoto* also appears in the *NS* and *KJ*.
[4] There is discussion on the meaning and etymology of the name 'Nakatomi' (中臣). As mentioned by Aston, the word can mean 'to mediate' (for example between the gods and men, heaven and earth), but it can also simply refer to the Chinese term 'middle minister.' While Aston prefers the second interpretation, the text above suggest that their function was seen as that of 'mediating' between men and gods. Aston, *Nihongi*, 1:42.

Kamatari was the eldest son of the official Mikeko and his mother was called Lady Ōtomo.[5] The Great Minister was born in the mansion of the wisteria fields in the first month of the thirty-fourth year of Heavenly Sovereign Toyomi Kekashiki.[6] Even while still inside Lady Ōtomo's womb, his cries could be heard from the outside. He was born after twelve months. Lady Ōtomo's mother spoke: "The number of months that you carried the child is different from what ordinary people experience. He will be an extraordinary child and certainly possess divine virtues." In her heart, Lady Ōtomo knew that this pregnancy had been different. Labour had been painless and without even realizing it she had given birth.

The Great Minister's character was benevolent and filial, his wisdom sharp and his knowledge of the arcane profound.[7] From a young age he liked studying and he became highly versed in historical writings. He often read Tai Gong's *Six Secret Teachings*, and there wasn't a single verse he could not repeat and recite.[8] His disposition was admirable and elegant and his posture was particularly noteworthy. When seen from the front, he appeared to be

---

[5] The identity of his father is also confirmed in the *Sonpi bunmyaku* where it is stated that Mikeko was the 'Great Ancestor of the Fujiwara' (藤原大祖是也) and lists him as son of Katanosa no Ōmuraji 可多能古大連 (?–?), a 17th generation descendant of the divine *Ame no Koyane no Mikoto*. *SB*, 22–27.

[6] Toyomi Kekashiki 豊御炊 refers to Suiko, a name also found in the *Kojiki* and the *Nihon Shoki*; *TK*, 124. 'Sovereign' here refers to 'tennō.'

[7] Literally the text states 'the arcane mirror is profound,' which is taken out of a passage from the *Huainanzi*: "A scholar who truly attains clear-minded understanding, who grasps the arcane mirror in his mind…will propound his writings and clarify his views." (誠得清明之士，執玄鑒於心，照物明白，不為古今易意，據書明指以示之，雖闔棺亦不恨矣) Adapted from Liu An, *The Huainanzi*, 786.

[8] The *Six Secret Teachings* or the *Liu Tao* (六韜) written by Tai Gong (太公), a military manual. Of note is the revolutionary character of this text since Kamatari will have to strategize and start a rebellion himself in 645. The *NS* does not explicitly mention the title of the text. Michael Como mentions that the text was transmitted to the Japanese (Yamato) court prior to Tenji's reign and its author was held in great esteem by its elite. Como, *Shōtoku, Ethnicity, Ritual and Violence in the Japanese Buddhist Tradition*, 202.

looking up; when seen from behind he appeared to be bowing.⁹ The Great Minister heard someone say, "Two valiant strong men follow him wherever he goes," and he became secretly embarrassed about himself. Those who are wise touch the heart and their fame steadily increases.

The sovereign's close advisor Soga no Kuratsukuri (宗我鞍作) had increased his own fortune and his power now permeated the court.¹⁰ When Kuratsukuri scolded and issued orders there was no one who didn't bend. However, when confronted with the Great Minister, he remained silent as he always considered him mysterious. Once, the nobles assembled in the hall of Master of the Dharma Min and read the part of the *Yijing* pertaining to the Zhou period.¹¹ The Great Minister arrived afterwards and Kuratsukuri stood up. He greeted the Great Minister and they sat together. When the lectures ended and everyone had returned, Master of the Dharma Min gave the minister a sign to stay. Then Master of the Dharma Min told the Great Minister:

---

⁹ 前看若偃後見如伏, *TK*, 129. The sentence implies he was a humble man.

¹⁰ 'Close advisor' refers to *kinshin* (近臣). The 'court' is the translation of *mikado* (朝); the *NS* mentions that Kuratsukuri conducted the *kokusei* (国政) or the 'policy of the country.' *NS* Kōgyoku 1 (642). 1; *TK*, 132.

¹¹ 'Master of the Dharma' (*hōshi* or *hofushi* 法師) Min (旻). The text referred to is the *Yijing* (here: *Zhou yi* 周易), the *NS* mentions that Kamatari studied Confucianism (周孔之教) under Minabuchi no Shōan 南淵請安 (?–?). NS Kōgyoku 3 (644).1; *TK* 131 and 133. The monk Min is mentioned in the *NS* as receiving the title of National Lecturer (*hakase*; 博士) in 645. Of Korean descent, he travelled to China in 608 and returned to Japan in 640. He is referred to as either 'Min' or 'Sōmin' (僧旻). There is no doubt he had a large influence at the court around this period and, as Bingenheimer pointed out, was said to be very knowledgeable about Confucian sources. His biography is also included in the *Honchō kōsō den* 本朝高僧伝. Bingenheimer, *A Biographical Dictionary…*, 125–127. Herman Ooms mentions that Min lectured on divination and criticized Soga no Emishi's role in government. Ooms, *Imperial Politics and Symbolics in Ancient Japan*, 89.

Among those who entered my hall, there is none like Soga no Tairō,[12] but your spiritual and knowledgeable appearance in reality supersedes this man. I beg you, be careful.[13]

Right after the onset of Okamoto Tennō's reign, the sons of noble families received silk caps, signifying their lineage inheritance.[14] The Great Minister refused, did not accept it and returned to Mishima for other tasks where he cultivated the Essence in nature.[15] People highly respected this. Suddenly, the Heavenly Sovereign Okamoto passed away and his consort ascended the throne.[16] The royal house fell into decline as she neglected the policy. The Great Minister lamented this.

At that time, Prince Karu suffered from an illness to his legs and was absent from the court.[17] The Great Minister had always

---

[12] Soga no Tairō or Kuratsukuri.

[13] As also pointed out by Go, the *NS* includes a passage from Kōgyoku 3 (644).1 in which it is mentioned that Nakatomi no Kamako (other name for Kamatari) met the later sovereign Tenji and that they studied the teachings of Confucius under a monk, probably Minabuchi no Shōan. Go identifies Shōan as a student of Min. *NS* Kōgyoku 3 (644); Go, "Nihon shoki to shunju kuyōden", 2–3; Aston vol. II, 184–185.

[14] Okamoto Tennō 岡本天皇 or Jomei Tennō 舒明天皇 (593–641).

[15] The *NS* also mentions that Kamatari stayed in Mishima (稱疾退居三島). *NS*, Kōgyoku 3 (644).1; Aston, vol. II, 184:'He declined the appointment several times...On the plea of ill health he went away and lived at Mishima'; *TK* 133. 'Cultivated the Essence in nature' (養素丘園) seems to stress Kamatari's involvement in religious and philosophical enquiry, to provide him with the necessary authority to act as one of the court's main officials. Okimura mentions that this could relate to Buddhist faith, but given prior reference to his study with the monk Min, I suggest this short sentence transcends Buddhism and refers to Chinese Learning. The very same sentence also occurs in several Chinese sources such as the *Bei shi* (北史) compiled between 630–650 by Li Yanshou (draft by Li Dashi). Wilkinson, *Chinese History: A New Manual*, 626–627; *TK* 136.

[16] The 'consort' (ōkisaki; 皇后) here is the female sovereign Kōgyoku. Okimura states she ascended the throne as 'tennō.' *TK*, 136. However, this term was not yet in use at the time and 'Ōkimi' (大君/大王) would have been used.

[17] Prince Karu (軽皇子), the later sovereign Kōtoku (孝徳; 596–654).

favoured the prince, so he went to the palace to stay by his side. Together they talked all night, forgetting their fatigue. Thus, Prince Karu knew the minister's ingenuity was great and that his knowledge surpassed the others. The Prince had his favourite consort serve and feed the minister morning and evening; his lodging, drink and food surpassed what normal people received. The Great Minister, sensing his favouritism, told a close attendant in confidence:

> The extraordinary favours that I have received well exceed what I had hoped for. Who wouldn't allow your master to become the sovereign?[18]

He stated he would not eat and would show his actions. The attendant passed this on to Prince Karu, who was very pleased. However, the prince's means were insufficient for such a great matter.[19]

If the Great Minister wanted to select someone from among the entire royal family, only Naka no Ōe was suitably ingenious and heroic, able to eliminate disorder.[20] However, there was no

---

[18] 'Sovereign' here is (帝皇) and read as *mikado* by Okimura, *TK*, 137. However, Bohner takes these characters in the reverse order (皇帝) and suggests *kōtei*. It is unclear why Bohner suggested this order, since the text used for his translation is the version contained in the Shinko gunsho ruijū 3, part 64, 1930 edition, which has '帝皇.' The version used by Okimura, in addition to the Edo period manuscript held by Waseda University Library, all have '帝皇'. Bohner, "Kamatari-Den," 228; *SGR* 3/64, 689; *TK*, 137.

[19] 'Great matter' is the translation for daiji (大事) and implicitly refers to the great matters of state.

[20] 'Ingenious' refers to yūryaku (雄略). This term appears in the *NS* as well and seems borrowed from several Chinese sources where it appears in connection with rebellion for the sake of the state or the sovereign. For example, in the History of the Later Han (*Hou Han shu*) it is stated that "Xun Yu heard that Cao possessed the ingenuity (to successfully suppress a revolt) and thus stopped Shao who he thought could not realize the great matters of state." (或聞操有雄略而度紹終不能定大業), Togashi, "Kanjin No Keifu," 5. The term can also be found in the name of the sovereign Yūryaku (5th

occasion for the Great Minister to meet him. By chance, he encountered him at the *kemari* court, when Naka no Ōe's shoe fell off through contact with the ball. The Great Minister took it up and presented it to him respectfully. Likewise, Naka no Ōe received it with respect.[21] From that moment, they were each other's friend and inseparable as fish and water.

In the tenth month of winter, in the second year of the later *Okamoto no Sumera no mikoto*, Soga no Iruka plotted with several princes, wishing to undermine Prince Kamitsumiya's son, Yamashiro no Ōe, and others, stating:

> Yamashiro no Ōe was born in my family.[22] Such a scent of brilliant virtue, the lingering of a holy event! When Okamoto Tennō ascended the throne, all ministers said there was strife between him and me. Following the murder of Sakahibe no Omi Marise, our hatred deepened.[23] Now, the Son of Heaven has passed away and his consort rules the court. Our hearts must be unsettled. How could there not be an uprising? I will no longer endure the intimate relation I had with my nephew Yamashiro; I will plan for the benefit of the state.

---

century). In the *Nihon Shoki*, the quality of *yūryaku* is ascribed to Sujin Tennō who had the military insight to eliminate disorder by sending out four generals. In addition, the text connects Sujin's ingenuity, a quality he possessed from childhood, with his ability to direct the matters of state, here rendered as 'tengyō' (天業): 識性聡敏幼好雄略。。。恒有経綸天業之心焉 (*The nature of consciousness was smart and quick and in his childhood he loved ingenuity* [to plan]...*He always ruled with a mind directed to the matters of Heaven*).

[21] As pointed out by Sakharova, this scene bares striking similarities with an episode from the *Han Shu* and the *Shih Ji* in which Zhang Liang offers a shoe to a Daoist master who dropped/tossed it intentionally from a bridge, seemingly to test the other's moral character. In addition, the Korean Samguk Sagi also refers to the king needing his ideal servant 'as much as a fish needs water', a statement also made after a piece of clothing is mended. Sakharova, *Fujiwara House Biography: Continental Prototypes*, 97.

[22] Prince Kamitsu miya the 'Prince of the Upper Palace' (*kamitsu miya no hitsugi no miko* 上宮太子) is Shōtoku Taishi.

[23] Sakahibe no Omi Marise 坂合部臣摩理勢; (?–?) and Yamashiro no Ōe had opposed Soga no Emishi, Iruka's father.

All of the princes thereupon consented, but agreed only from fear of his reprisal. Several months and days later, Yamashiro no Ōe was assassinated at Ikaruga Temple.[24] Those who learned about it grieved. Kuratsukuri's father, Great Minister Toyura, was indignant:

> Kuratsukuri, where could we find an insane man like you?[25] Our lineage will perish. I am lamenting and feel defeated.

Kuratsukuri said:

> We have already deboned the fish; there is no place for remorse.

It gradually became apparent at the court that the once-tranquil Han had fallen into disarray and the savagery and arrogance of Dong Zhuo had appeared in the country.[26]
Thereupon Naka no Ōe addressed the Great Minister:

> The policy of the monarch is carried out by her counsellor, as if Zhou's tripod cauldron has been transferred to the Li.[27] What do you think of this? Please, describe your ingenious plans.

---

[24] The murder is also mentioned in the *NS*, Kōgyoku 2 (643).11.

[25] Great Minister Toyura (豊浦大臣) is Soga no Emishi. The *NS* does not use 'Toyura' but 'Emishi.' *TK*, 149; *NS* Kōgyoku 2 (643).11.

[26] Dong Zhuo 董卓 (?–192) was a warlord who marched into the fallen capital Luoyang in 189 after the death of the Han Emperor Lingdi 靈帝 (156–189), marking the last stable period of the Han dynasty (206 BC–220 AD). He briefly filled a power vacuum from Ch'ang An from where he controlled the court around 191. After his assassination the Emperor reached Luoyang again by 196 when the official Cao Cao 曹操 (155–220) took control of the court. Beck, "The Fall of Han," 340–350. Bohner interprets '安漢' as a proper name, referring to 安漢公, an epithet for Wang Mang 王莽 (33 BC–23 AD) However, this does not fit the chronology of the Later Han. Bohner, "Kamatari-Den," 229.

[27] The Li (李氏) refers to *Jisun* (季孫) a powerful clan of the state of Lu (魯国) during the Spring and Autumn period and one of three clans that brought about the collapse of Lu. *TK*, 152. The cauldron (鼎) was a ritual vessel symbolizing the sovereignty of a given dynasty.

The Great Minister related in detail his plot to eliminate disorder and return to the correct way.[28] Naka no Ōe was delighted and spoke:

> You are indeed my Zhang Liang![29]

The Great Minister wished to seek the support of the powerful houses, in secret looked for Kuratsukuri's weakness and learned of envy between Yamada no Omi and Kuratsukuri. He explained to Naka no Ōe:

> If one observes Yamada no Omi's character, he is firm and enduring, skilled and daring; his power and expectations are high.[30] If you are able to gain his consent, the rebellion should certainly succeed. Please, first draw him close through marriage, and afterwards you should talk to him about the plot we have devised.

Naka no Ōe complied and asked for the hand of the daughter of the house of Minister Yamada, who consented.

In the third month of spring, when a hundred carriages went out to meet them, Muzashi abducted the bride and took off.[31]

---

[28] 'To eliminate disorder and return to the correct way' (撥乱反正) is a concept paraphrased from the main commentary on the Spring and Autumn Annals, the *Chunqiu Gongyang Zhuan* (春秋公羊傳), though the expression also occurs in the *Shiji* (史記) and the *Hanyu* (漢書). For example the idea appears in chapter twenty-eight of the *Chunqiu Gongyang Zhuan*, in the annals of Duke Ai, see Miller trans., *Chunqiu Gongyang Zhuan*, 275.

[29] The characters 'shibau' (子房) here refer to the Han period official Zhang Liang (張良;?–186 BC) who was a close (Daoist) advisor to Gaozu (高祖; Original name: Liu Bang), the first Emperor of the Han Dynasty. Of note here is Zhang Liang's biography in book 55 of Sima Qian's *Shiji*. In this text, we encounter the famous passage in which Zhang Liang puts Huang Shigong's shoe back on, an episode that might have influenced the *Kamatari-den*'s scene in which Kamatari returns Naka no Ōe's shoe.

[30] Minister Yamada (山田臣) is *Soga no Kurayamada no Iskikawa Maro* (蘇我倉山田石川麻呂) as mentioned in the *NS*, Kōgyoku 3 (644).1.

[31] The abduction is also mentioned in the *NS*, Kōgyoku 3 (644).1; The *TK* mentions she was abducted by '武蔵,' interpreted as 'Muzashi'

Yamada no Omi was distressed and afraid, not knowing what had to be done. His younger daughter was at his side, saw her father's grieving complexion and asked: "Why are you so sad?" Her father explained his reasons. His younger daughter said:

> I might not possess Xi Shi's complexion but I do have the spirit of Mo Mu.[32] Please, choose me and offer me for marriage.

Her father was delighted and eventually presented his younger daughter. Naka no Ōe was upset about Muzashi's disrespect and wanted to carry out the death penalty. The Great Minister advised him:

> A great matter under Heaven has been settled, why be angry about a small matter that occurred in your house?[33]

Naka no Ōe thereupon gave up his intentions.[34]

---

by Okimori. *TK*, 155. However, the characters used in the *NS* are different: '身狹' and the pronunciation given is 'Musa' (complete title Musa no Omi). His full name was Soga no Musa 蘇我武蔵.

[32] Xi Shi (西施) was said to have been a beauty who lived during the Spring and Autumn Period; Mo Mu (嫫姆) was the fourth wife of the Yellow Emperor (黄帝). *TK*, 156. Both also appears in the *Huainanzi*, where the present text clearly draws from: "[The ugly] Mo Mu had some beautiful points. [The Great beauty] Xi Shi had some ugly points" (嫫母有所美, 西施有所醜) Liu An, *The Huainanzi*, 655.

[33] 'A great matter under Heaven' refers to '天下之大事,' a prerequisite of which is the characteristic of 'ingenuity' (*yūryaku*) or '雄略,' a word mentioned earlier in the Chronicle when Prince Karu is described as not having this talent, meaning he is unfit to rule the realm.

[34] Naka no Ōe took Yamada no Omi's other daughter, Soga no Ochi no Iratsume 蘇我遠智娘, instead as consort, an alliance that would end in bloodshed in 649. In a conflict based on accusations of treason against the sovereign voiced by Soga no Himuka (another name for Muzashi), Soga no Kurayamada no Iskikawa Maro would commit suicide at *Yamadadera* along with eight of his children in 649. However, after his death his innocence was proven and he was posthumously exonerated. Soga no Ochi no Iratsume died shortly afterwards, probably by taking her own life after the suicides and

Afterwards, the Great Minister calmly explained to Yamada no Omi:

> Soga no Iruka's violent opposition is hated by both men and gods. If this evil continues, certainly misfortune will wipe out his clan. Please observe the situation cautiously.

Yamada no Omi said:

> I concur. I will respectfully follow your orders.

They both agreed on a strategy and then wished to assemble soldiers. Naka no Ōe said:

> I fear this plan will not succeed if we announce our intentions. But if we do not announce it, then the sovereign may be disturbed.[35] How can the Principle of the subject be in accordance with Righteousness? May you and Minister Yamada explain it to me.

The Great Minister replied:

> The actions of her subject consist of Loyalty and Piety.[36] The Way of Loyalty and Piety unifies the country and brings prosperity to the clans. To allow for the sovereign's line to be cut off and allow for its foundations to be shattered and destroyed...It is not filial and not loyal to not proceed with this revolt.

Naka no Ōe spoke:

---

execution of most of her family. Ebersole, *Ritual Poetry,* 223–227. The NS mentions the following poignant episode, when Yamada no Ōmi exclaims: "I have now been slandered by Musashi (here: 身刺), and I fear that I shall be unjustly put to death. With so near a prospect of the yellow springs, I would withdraw from life, still cherishing fidelity in my bosom..." Aston, *Nihongi,* 4:233; NS Taika 5 (649).3.

[35] 'Sovereign' is here the translation of 'sumeramikoto' (帝), referring to the female monarch Kōgyoku (皇極), Naka no Ōe's mother.

[36] Referring to Naka no Ōe's duties of loyalty (忠) as her (the sovereign's) subject and filiality (孝) as her son. *TK,* 160.

Our success or loss depends on you. You should act with effort.

Then, the Great Minister recommended Saeki no Muraji Komaro and Waka Inukai no Muraji Amita, saying:

"They are courageous and strong, and their strength will lift the cauldron.[37] What should be done for the greater good of the state can be left to just these two men.

Naka no Ōe followed his advice.

In the sixth month of the summer in the fourth year of the later Okamoto no sumeramikoto, Naka no Ōe pretended that a declaration of the Three Korean Kingdoms had to be proclaimed in front of the sovereign and people believed this to be true.[38] Then, he said to Yamada no Omi:

I will have you read the declaration of the Three Kingdoms. We intend to take advantage of Iruka's negligence and murder him.

Yamada no Omi agreed. Thus, the plan was established.

On the twelfth day, the sovereign proceeded towards the seat of governance.[39] Furubito no Ōe was in attendance.[40] A chamberlain

---

[37] Saeki no Muraji Komaro 佐伯連古麻呂 (?–?) and Waka Inukai no Muraji Amita 稚犬養連網田 (?–?) are also mentioned in the *NS*, Kōgyoku 3 (644).1. The expression 'to lift the cauldron' (扛鼎) is found in several Chinese sources such as the *Shiji* and indicates extreme strength (to support the state). *TK*, 158.

[38] '…in the fourth year of the later *Okamoto no sumeramikoto*' (後岡本天皇) refers to Kōgyoku 4 (645). The three Korean kingdoms are Koguryŏ (高句麗), Paekche (百済) and Silla (新羅).

[39] *tsuchinoe saru* (戊申). The same date is confirmed in the NS for that day where it is stated that the sovereign proceeded to the *Great Hall of State* or *Daigokuden* (大極殿). *TK*, 164. *NS*, 263.

[40] Furubito no Ōe 古人大兄; (?–?) was the grandson of Soga no Umako 蘇我馬子; (?–626) and half-brother of Naka no Ōe (both were sons of Jomei through different mothers). Ebersole, *Ritual Poetry*, 224–225. The *NS* confirms he was in attendance. NS Kōgyoku 4 (645). 6. Originally he was Soga no Emishi's preferred candidate to become

was sent to quickly summon Iruka. Iruka stood up and started to put on his shoes but even after three times was not able to put them on. In his mind, Iruka was distracted and he hesitated, thinking about returning. The Great Minister knew from before that Iruka was very suspicious and that he carried a sword from morning till evening. Therefore he had already taught an entertainer ways to remove it from him. Iruka smiled and untied his sword. He entered, sat down and waited.[41]

Yamada no Omi proceeded to read the declaration of the Three Kingdoms. Suddenly, Naka no Ōe ordered the guards of the gates to simultaneously close the twelve entrance gates to the palace. Then, Naka no Ōe grabbed the long spear he had previously hidden on the side of the hall. The Great Minister was armed with bow and arrow to provide him cover. He had ordered for two swords to be placed in a box for Saeki no Muraji Komaro and Waka Inukai no Muraji Amita and said:

With full force, stab him once and kill him.

They drank water with their meal, swallowed, and then vomited from apprehension. The Great Minister raised his voice to embolden them.

When the declaration was about to end, Yamada no Omi became afraid because Komaro and the others had not yet arrived. Sweat ran down his body, his voice trembled and his hands were shaking. Kuratsukuri found this strange and asked: "Why are you afraid? Why do you shudder?" Yamada no Omi said: "Waiting close to the throne, I did not realize I was sweating." Seeing that Komaro and the others feared Iruka's might and were not closing in, Naka no Ōe exclaimed: "Ya!" With Komaro he leapt out, surprising Iruka, and they injured him on his head and shoulder. Startled, Iruka rose. Komaro turned his hand, brandished his sword and cut Iruka's leg. Iruka stood up, approached the throne, kowtowed and said:

---

sovereign, but instead Jomei's first consort ascended the throne as Kōgyoku. Furuhito entered the priesthood after Iruka's assassination.

[41] The *Kamatari-den* borrowed, or at times paraphrases, this section (From 'On the 12th day' to '...waited') from the *NS*, with some adjustments in the details of the account. *NS* Kōgyoku 4 (645). 6.

"Your servant knows of no crime. I request, ask them for an explanation." The sovereign was shocked and she addressed Naka no Ōe: "What is happening? Explain yourself!" Naka no Ōe threw himself on the floor and proclaimed:

> Kuratsukuri is completely extinguishing the royal house and he will overthrow the position of the heavenly sovereign. How can we replace the son of Heaven with Kuratsukuri?

The sovereign rose and withdrew into the palace's quarters. Komaro and the others then finished off Kuratsukuri. That day it rained. Pouring water overflowed the garden. Kuratsukuri's corpse was covered with a paper screen.[42]

According to the opinion at the time the traitor was killed in accordance with Heaven. However, Iruka's father Toyura no Ōmi remained, and the dishonest thieves were not yet subdued.[43] Consequently the sovereign and her entourage entered Hōkōji, used it as their stronghold and prepared for the unexpected. The nobility and the counsellors all followed. A messenger handed over Kuratsukuri's corpse to Toyura no Ōmi.

Thereupon, Aya no Atahi and others assembled their entire clan, set up camp, armoured and prepared soldiers to help the Great Minister.[44] Naka no Ōe had Kose no Omitokoda proclaim:

> Our state affairs do not depend on you. Why do you distance yourselves from Heaven and rebel? Do you seek the collapse of your family?[45]

Takamuku no Omikunioshi of the rebelling party spoke to Aya no Atahi and the others:

---

[42] A visual depiction of the event, with Soga no Iruka's body covered with mats in the rain, can be seen in the 16th century *Tōnomine Engi Emaki*.

[43] Toyura no Ōomi (豊浦大臣) refers to Soga no Emishi, Iruka's father.

[44] Aya no Atahi (漢直;?–?) is mentioned in the NS as performing duties as a guard for Soga no Emishi, NS Kōgyoku 3 (644).11; *TK*, 180.

[45] Kose no Ōmi Tokoda (巨勢臣徳陀; 592–658) reached the high rank of Great Minister of the Left (sadaijin; 左大臣) in Taika 5 (649). 4.20 under Kōtoku Tennō; *KB* Taika 5 (649); *NS* Saimei 4 (658). 1.

Our Lord Tairō has already been murdered. Our Great Minister in vain awaited his execution. For whom did we fight in vain?[46]

Having spoken, he withdrew and fled. The thieves retreated and dispersed.

On the thirteenth day, Toyura no Ōmi Emishi committed suicide at his mansion; the foul stench of treachery was washed away and the wolves had been discarded.[47] The people rejoiced and danced, with everyone shouting: "Ten thousand years!" Naka no Ōe praised:

> The continuous line has been restored. Truly, your strength is what saved its fate from destruction.

The minister spoke:

> I did everything based upon your holy virtue. It is not my achievement, your humble subject.

All conceded that their success was not through their own effort.

On the fourteenth day, Heavenly Sovereign *Ame Toyotakara Ikashishi Tarashi Hime* desired to transfer the throne to Naka no Ōe.[48] Naka no Ōe consulted with the Great Minister and he replied:

---

[46] Takamuku no Ōmi Kunioshi (高向臣国押; ?–?) He was involved in an attempt to arrest Yamashiro no Ōe as ordered by Iruka in 643; *NS* Kōgyoku 2 (643). 11; *TK*, 182.

[47] *tsuchi no tonotori*; 己酉 ; *Toyura no Ōmi Emishi* Soga no Emishi's suicide is also described in the NS in much more detail. This text adds that before his death, the *History of the Sovereigns* (天皇記) and the *History of the Country* (国記) were burnt. It is also added that permission was given to bury him in a tomb. *NS* Kōgyoku 4 (645).6.

[48] *tsuchi no kanoe inu*; 庚戌; 'Heavenly Sovereign' refers to *sumeramikoto* (天皇). *Ame Toyotakara Ikashishi Tarashi Hime* (天豊財重日足姫) refers to the former female sovereign Kōgyoku who will become sovereign again as Saimei (斉明; r. 655–661) after the death of Kōtoku (孝徳 ; r. 645–654).

Furubito no Ōe is your older brother. Karu no Mantoku no Ō is your uncle from mother's side.⁴⁹ If indeed now you bypass Furubito no Ōe and you ascend the throne of the sovereign, then the people will perceive this as unlike the respectful, humble heart of a younger brother. Thus, would it be possible to decide on your uncle in accordance with the will of the people?

Naka no Ōe followed this and in secret explained it to the sovereign.

In accordance with the plan, the sovereign abdicated the throne to Prince Karu, who became Ameyorozu Toyohi no Sumeramikoto.⁵⁰ This truly was the original intention of the Great Minister. The wise said:

> We have seen today that you do not break your word." Ame Toyotakara Ikashihi no Sumeramikoto will be granted the name *Sumemi Oya no Mikoto* and Naka no Ōe will become the Crown Prince.⁵¹ The period of reign will be changed into 'Taika.'

The sovereign stated:

> The protection and safety of the realm depends on your strength. You unified the axis of chariots and scrolls in this revolt. I bestow upon you the large brocade cap and the rank of minister of the interior, receiving two thousand households. The affairs of the military and the country are assigned to your position.

The Great Minister inspected the forests and bushes, and the work of the common people. People attended their responsibilities and no fields were left to fallow. The nine offices functioned without obstacles and the five ranks all were in harmony.

---

49 Karu no Mantoku no Ō (軽万徳王).
50 The term for sovereign here is *mikado* (帝). *Ameyorozu Toyohi no Sumeramikoto* (天万豊日天皇) refers to Kōtoku.
51 *Sumemi Oya no Mikoto* (皇祖母尊), see also NS Kōtoku, *sokui zenki*. As kindly suggested by Ross Bender, the term can also be interpreted as 'imperial ancestor.'

In the eight month of autumn of Hakuhō 5 (654), the sovereign declared:

> To revere the Way and appoint the wise has been the eternal law of former sovereigns. To praise achievements and reward virtue has been the instruction of the sage. The virtue of the Minister of the Interior *Nakatomi no Muraji* with the large brocade cap is equal to *Take no uchi no Sukune*, but his position does not yet correspond to the will of the people.[52] Therefore I bestow upon him the purple cap and increase his reward to eight thousand households.[53]

Suddenly *Ameyorozu Toyohi no Sumeramikoto*, already tired of governance, ascended to the white clouds.[54] Her highness and mother of the sovereign *Sumemi Oya no Mikoto* again entered the jeweled era following general request and entrusted all matters of governance to the crown prince.[55] The crown prince decided each matter after consultation and then carried it out. He crossed seas, climbed mountains, and appreciation for the court flowed continuously. There were more and more villages where the people stomped the earth and hit their bellies like drums. If it wasn't for the Great Minister's holiness and intelligence, how could we have attained this splendour? Therefore, he was promoted to the rank of Large Purple Cap and received the position of 'kō.'[56] His households were increased by five thousand; he now held approximately fifteen thousand households.

---

[52] *Take no uchi no Sukune* (建内宿禰) is a mythical 'ideal' servant who is said to have descended from the (mythical) sovereign Kōgen (孝元). He appears in the Kojiki. TK, 195 and also served Jingu Kōgō and Ōjin Tennō.

[53] It is not clear when Kamatari received the Purple Cap (*murasaki no kagafuri* 紫冠). Kamatari strictly speaking did not yet have the necessary rank (*daijin* 大臣) to receive the Purple Cap in 654. He did not attain this position until 669.

[54] Kōtoku passed away in Hakuchi 5 (654).10 ; 'governance' is the translation for *matsurigoto* (万機).

[55] This sentence refers to former sovereign Kōgyoku taking the throne again as Saimei.

[56] Historically, it is unclear when he was promoted. The conferral of the rank 'ko' (公) is not included in the *NS*. See *TK*, 200.

In the tenth month of the winter of the twelfth year, the sovereign proceeded to the Naniwa palace.[57] Thereupon, in accordance with what was requested by Fukushin, she proceeded to Tsukushi, dispatched auxiliary troops, and began preparations for military provision.[58] In the first month of spring in the thirteenth year, the fleet moved to the West. First, they headed to Umitsumichi. In the third month, the fleet arrived at Na no Ōtsu, and the sovereign stayed at the Iwase Kari Palace. She changed the Palace's name and called it Nagatsu. In the fifth month of summer, the sovereign moved, and she stayed at the Asakura no Tachibana no Hironiwa Palace, where she oversaw foreign policy.

When the seventh month of autumn arrived, the health of the sovereign deteriorated. The Great Minister harboured fear in his heart and prayed to the gods. Relying on the Three Regalia he ardently sought her longevity. He was blessed by a statue of the Buddha who appeared to reach out his arm; as if in a dream Kannon herself appeared in the air. The apparition of holiness was palpable. Therefore, the monk Dōken said:

> In the past, members of the guard requested to die when the axis of the wheel turned. At the moment the monarch died, righteous sons tore open the earth to bury themselves.[59] Clouds of birds concealed the sun and the ministers prayed with their whole bodies.[60] The gods of the rivers were cursed, and counsellors sought their own sacrifice. Although your beautiful name will not wither and your honour and sincerity will become increasingly fragrant, today is different. How can we say that the present is similar to the days of yore?

---

[57] Female sovereign Saimei.
[58] 'Fukushin' is the Japanese reading for Kwisil Pok-sin (Jap.: Kishitsu Fukushin 鬼室福信; ?–663). He was originally from Paekche and was beheaded in 663 by 'King' (王) Puyŏ P'ung of Puyŏ (扶余豊璋); NS, Tenji 2 (663).6.
[59] Dōken (道顕) was a monk from Koguryŏ (高句麗) and the author of the Nihon seiki 日本世記. A fragment of this source quoted in the NS suggests that he was close to Kamatari. TK, 207. NS Tenji 8 (669).10.
[60] This sentence refers to the Shiji and the Chunqiu Zuo Zhuan (春秋左傳), TK, 207–208. 'Ministers' is the translation for ling yin (令尹).

Her life had reached its limit, and the monarch passed away in the Asakura no Kari Palace. The Crown Prince put on mourning garb and took over the polity.[61] That month, General Su and the Turkut Prince Qibi Heli arrived at Koguryŏ's stronghold through both land and sea routes.[62] The Crown Prince moved to the Nagatsu palace where he stayed and continued to oversee foreign military policy.

At that time he spoke to his personal attendants:

> I have heard that 'The Great Tang had Wei Zheng, Koguryŏ had Kae Kim, Paekche had Song Chung, and Silla had Su Sun.'[63] Each one protected their state and their fame reached ten thousand li. These were all great men in their country, and their wisdom and strategy surpassed ordinary men. Compared to our Minister of the Interior, these people would reach below his middle. How could they compete with him?

Until the eleventh month of winter, the Crown Prince mourned; the remains of the deceased sovereign were moved from Asakura Palace and interred in Asuka Kahara.[64]

In the fourteenth year, the Crown Prince became regent. Having gone through hardships from a young age, the friendship between him and the Great Minister only became more profound. Despite being lord and vassal in principle, they were friend and teacher in conduct. When they went out, they rode horses side-by-side or shared a carriage. Inside, their cushions touched and their knees were close. Their policy combined simplicity and quietness, and in their cultural refinement there was benevolence

---

[61] The 'Crown Prince' is here the future sovereign Tenji.

[62] General Su (蘇将軍) refers to Su Dingfang 蘇定方 (?-?), a Tang general who defeated Turkic forces; Prince Qibi Heli (突厥王子契苾加力) originally led the Turkic Qibi tribe but submitted to the Tang in 632. He then went on to serve Emperor Taizong and he is often portrayed as the ideal military servant. His lord (Taizong) treated him benevolently and in return Heli offered him loyalty. Skaff, *Sui-Tang China and Its Turko-Mongol Neighbors*, 100–101. *TK*, 211.

[63] Wei Zheng (魏徵; 580–643); Kae Kim (蓋金) appears in a fragment of the *Nihon seiki* in the *NS* Tenji 3 (664).10; Song Chung (善仲); Su Sun (鵂淳).

[64] 'Sovereign' refers here to *sumeramikoto* (天皇).

and wisdom. Eventually, their virtue spread in the country and their influence spread overseas. Thus, the three kingdoms served the regent and the ten thousand clans were at peace.

The king of Koguryŏ sent a letter to the Minister of the Interior:

> I believe that the Great Minister's wind of benevolence blows from afar, and his immense virtue stretches widely. You declare the sovereign will instruct the people for a thousand years, and his fragrant scent will spread ten thousand li. You became the pillar of the state and constructed floating bridges among its people. You are admired by the entire country and you are wanted by the common people. People hear you from afar and clap their hands out of joy. Their happiness spreads and truly deepens.

In the third month of spring of the sixth year of the regency, the capital was moved to nearby Ōmi.[65] In the first month of the seventh year, the sovereign ascended the throne.[66] He became *Amemikoto Hirakasu Wake no sumeramikoto*.[67] There were no bad omens at court and the surroundings looked fine. The people experienced no famines and the households had more than enough provisions. The entire populace called it a period of great peace.

The sovereign invited his ministers and held a banquet in his beach pavilion. The wine was pleasing and enjoyment reached great heights. Suddenly, the younger brother of the sovereign took a long spear and spiked it though a wooden plank.[68] The sovereign was baffled, became enraged and was about to punish and kill his brother. The Great Minister firmly cautioned him; the sovereign consequently stopped. When they first met, the younger brother

---

[65] Also mentioned in the *NS*, along with the opposition against the move of the capital, *NS* Tenji 6 (667).3: 是時、天下百姓不願遷都; *TK*, 220.
[66] *NS* Tenji 7 (668).1.
[67] *Amemikoto Hirakasu Wake no sumeramikoto* 天命開別天皇.
[68] The 'younger brother of the sovereign' (大皇弟) is Ōama no ōji (大海人皇子), the later sovereign Tenmu. Torquil Duthie discusses this passage to show that the Fujiwara narrative is not directed against Tenmu, who is here depicted as being favourable towards Kamatari. Duthie, "The Jinshin Rebellion and the Politics of Historical Narrative in Early Japan", 316.

of the sovereign feared the Great Minister because of his high position. After meeting, he came to considerably value the Minister, like a parent. Later, at the time of the Jinshin rebellion, when he headed to Atsuma from Yoshino he lamented:

> If the Minister had still been alive, would we be in this trouble?

This is what people thought.

In the ninth month of autumn of the seventh year, Silla sent tribute. The Great Minister reciprocated by gifting the high official of Silla a ship, through the official Kim Tong Won.[69] Someone objected and the Great Minister replied:

> All under Heaven must be Tenji's land. The guests within its boundaries must be the sovereign's servants.

Before this, the sovereign had ordered the Great Minister to dictate court etiquette and issue legal codes.[70] Based on the nature of Heaven and men he composed the court's code of conduct. The Minister and the wise men of the time determined the disadvantages and advantages of the old scriptures and drafted brief legal articles. He revered the way of respectful affection, and likewise blocked the path towards wickedness. The principle consisted of discretion in judging and sentencing, the virtue consisted of love for living beings. From the Three Classics of the Zhou to the Nine Chapters of the Han, nothing was changed.[71]

---

[69] The official Kim Tong Won (金東厳) is also mentioned in the *NS* Tenji 7 (668).9; *TK*, 125.

[70] The legal codes mentioned here underscore not just Kamatari's importance, but provide a direct link with Fujiwara no Fuhito who drafted the *Yōrō ritsuryō* (養老律令) that were on their turn implemented by Fujiwara no Nakamaro. The purpose of this statement is to underscore the unbroken line Kamatari-Fuhito-Nakamaro.

[71] 至於周之三典、漢之九篇 refers to the Zhou's three legal codes being the Qing dian (軽典), Zhong dian (中典) and Zhong dian (重典), consisting of penal codes for a new country (新国), a country at peace (平国) and a country facing rebellion (乱国). As pointed out

In the tenth month of winter in the second year after the ascension of the sovereign, the Great Minister weakened, became ill and finally his illness turned dire. The sovereign proceeded to the Minister's private residence and inquired about his condition.[72] He pleaded to the divine Shang-di for his life and searched the Minister for signs of improvement. The pledging and requesting had no effect, and the following day the illness had become heavier. Thereupon the sovereign stated:

If you are thinking about something, then I should hear it.

The Great Minister replied:

Your servant cannot be prompt now, what could I even say? However, regarding my funeral, I request simplicity. In life, I did not gain military honour, why should my death result in travail for the people?

Then, lying down, the Great Minister fell silent. The sovereign's throat choked; distressed, he could not control himself. He returned to the palace.

The sovereign sent his younger brother, the crown prince of the eastern palace, to his house to state:[73]

When one reflects upon previous ages from a distance, then across time and generations there were more than one or two servants of a sovereign who conducted policy. However, if one considers the accomplishments of their efforts, they did not do

---

by Okimori, this statement might have been inspired by the *Zhou Li* (周礼); *TK*, 227. The 'nine chapters of the Han' might refer to a set of legal codes based on the three codes originally established by the patriarch of the Han Dynasty.

[72] The exemplary conduct of a sovereign visiting his ill servant can also be found in continental sources, such as the Samguk Sagi. Sakharova, *Fujiwara House Biography: Continental Prototypes*, 101.

[73] The 'younger brother, crown prince of the eastern palace' (東宮大皇弟) refers to Prince Ōama no ōji. This passage also occurs in the *NS* Tenji 8 (669).10.

as well as you did. It is not merely we who have affection for you. Sovereigns of later generations will truly bless your descendants. Not forgetting and not dismissing, they will acknowledge your good deeds widely and deeply. Having heard your sickness has become heavier, our hearts hurt more and more. We confer upon you the rank you should hold.

Then, Great Minister Kamatari received the brocade cap, was appointed Dajōdaijin and his line became the 'Fujiwara Asomi.'[74]

On the sixteenth day, Kamatari passed away at the residence at Afumi. At that time, he was fifty-six years old.[75] The sovereign wept and was highly distressed. Court was suspended for nine days. On the nineteenth, he sent Soga no Toneri no Omi to state:

> The Inner Palace Minister Asomi passed away unexpectedly.[76] Why does the blue Heaven take away our good men? How painful! How Sad! Leaving us behind, he now is far away. Unfathomable! Regretful! He is now estranged from us, separated for eternity. What to say and not to say at your demise? This is no metaphor, this is reality. Day and night we led each other by hand, you acted as a friend and were appointed my messenger. Our hearts were at peace. There is no doubt about what you said and what you did. You decided on the sovereign's small and great matters.[77] The eight directions are still and tranquil and the thousand peoples are without distress.[78] These words

---

[74] The conferral of the the name 'Fujiwara' and his rank are also mentioned in the NS Tenji 8 (669).10. See also the SB, 6. The honorary title 'Asomi' (朝臣) was part of the kabane (姓)rank system possibly formed in the 5th century but adapted by Temmu in 684. See Piggott, *The Emergence of Japanese Kingship*, 314. Dajōdaijin' or 'Prime Minister' as translated by John W. Hall and Jeffrey P. Mass, eds., *Medieval Japan: Essays in Institutional History*, 54.

[75] The date is confirmed in the NS, adding a quote from the *Nihon seiki* in which his age is mentioned ('fifty-sixth Spring and Autumns'), NS Tenji 8 (669).10.

[76] Soga no Toneri no Omi (宗我舎人臣;); the 16th or 甲子 (kinoe-ne).

[77] 'Sovereign' for '国家.'

[78] This is an allusion to a passage from the *Huainanzi*: " Unless he is calm and indifferent, he will not be able to shine forth his Moral Potency. Unless he is still and tranquil, he will not be able to extend

are too miserable and narrow and do not do you justice. Oh! What should we do? You presented explanations in the palace for the people's own benefit. You argued about the policy in the tents of the military, and we certainly agreed. Truly, this only happens once in a thousand years. King Wen appointed Shang Fu and the founder of the Han had Zhang Liang as his minister. Isn't this just like the two of us?[79] We held hands from morning till evening, affectionate and never bored. We left and entered the same cart, and when we went out, etiquette was followed. Not yet having crossed the great river, the boat and the wheel have already sunk. The foundation and the beams of the large house that is the state have broken. With whom shall we direct the country, with whom shall we govern the people? Each time I reflect upon this, my sadness cuts even deeper. However, I have heard that even the great enlightened ones cannot avoid this. Therefore my pain and grief are somewhat consoled, enabling me to feel peace and tranquility. If the dead have spirits, then I believe you can see the prior sovereign and his consort.[80] Please tell them: "O prior sovereigns, on tranquil days you enjoy the scenery at the Afumi and Hira no Ura Palace, just like in the days of yore.[81] Each time we see this, our eyes hurt and our hearts are in pain. Not one step we forget, not a single word we discard. When we look up we see the virtue of your wisdom, when we look down, our longing for your affection deepens. In addition, since you have

---

his rule to distant places" （是故非澹薄無以明德，非寧靜無以致遠）. Liu An, *The Huainanzi*, 317.

[79] This refers to the founding of the Zhou dynasty ca. 1059 by King Wen (文王;), though modern scholarship has the Zhou start from Wen's successor Wu. Wilkinson 688. Okimori points out that the 状 and 兼 versions of the Chronicle provide '父' instead of '文,' *TK*, 241; Shang Fu (尚父) is Jiang Shang (姜尚), a military strategist employed by King Wen. Bohner translates this literally as 'Father Shang' (Vater Shang), Bohner, "Kamatari-Den," 242; The 'founder of the Han' (漢祖) was Liu Bang (劉邦; ?–195BC) who originally held the title of 'King of Han' (漢王) from 206 BC, Wilkinson, *Chinese History*, 704.

[80] In this case the prior sovereign [here: *mikado* (帝)] is Jomei and his consort was Kōgyoku (Saimei).

[81] Afumi (淡海) and Hira no Ura Palace (平浦宮) were located on the western bank of Lake Biwa. The presence of this sovereign and his consort at this site is confirmed in the *NS* Saimei 5 (659).3. *TK*, 245.

left the household and returned to the Buddha, surely you need the ritual implements of the Dharma. Therefore, we offer you a pure golden incense stand. With this stand, you, as if praying, will arrive at Tusita Heaven after having followed Kannon Bosatsu and day after day, night after night, you will listen to the marvelous preaching of Maitreya. Morning after morning and evening after evening you will turn the Dharma Wheel of Thusness.

The highest court aristocrats, the counsellors and the hundred bureaucrats all proceeded to the hall of spirits and mourned, followed by the funerary cart and its guards. The Great Minister was covered with drapes of feathers, followed by musicians beating drums and playing flutes. On the day of the funeral, the procession passed by the palace. The sovereign wore mourning garb and walked along. He ordered that the mourning chants cease, turned towards the funerary cart, cried bitterly and wept. Since ancient times, such expressions of gratitude from a sovereign and such high affection from his officials had never taken place. Based on the Great Minister's own words, the means for burial were carried out in a humble manner, expressing his final wish.

Then, on the sixth day of the ninth month of the year of *kōgo* (670) Kamatari was cremated at his mansion at Yamashina.[82] By imperial order, the princes, higher nobility and soldiers gathered at the burial site. Lower Large Brocade *Ki no Ushi no Omi* was ordered to state the final words and fulfil the obligation of funerary offerings.[83] At that time, the clouds in the sky formed a purple radiance. The sounds of strings and flutes above could be heard. A large gathering heard and saw this and lamented that this had not yet taken place before. It was the Great Minister's character to honour the Three Jewels. He revered them and spread them in the four directions. Each year in the tenth month, he erected

---

[82] Several sources related to early Kōfukuji connect Yamashina (山階) with Kamatari. In addition, passages of the *Kōfukuji ryūki* designate a private temple at this site as Kōfukuji's predecessor, referred to as *Yamashina dera*. The cremation is not mentioned in the *NS*.

[83] *Ki no Ushi no Omi* (紀大人臣; ?–?), in the *NS* he is mentioned to have been included among the *gyō shi taifu* (御史大夫; also: *dainagon*, 大納言) in 671, *NS* Tenji 10 (671).1; *TK*, 252.

a platform to expound the Dharma, to revere the Great Way of the Vimalakīrti Sūtra, and expound the marvelous principle of non-duality.[84] In addition, the possessions of his household were divided and deposed at Gangōji, to enhance the study of the Five Teachings. Thus the lineage of eminent priests was not cut off and the Way of the Holy One prospered. How could these not be signs?

There was a man from Paekche named Sataku Seimei with the rank of Lesser Purple Cap who was unrivalled in talent and thinking, and during his life the foremost in composition.[85] He was pained that the Great Minister's reputation was not passed on, that his wisdom and virtue would hollow out and perish. Therefore he composed an epithet, now included in a different work. Great Minister Kamatari had two sons, Jōe and Fuhito. Fuhito is included in another chronicle.

□

The Chronicle of Jōe 貞慧伝[86]

Jōe was wise in character and he loved to study. The Great Minister considered him different but, despite being as hard as steel,

---

[84] This most likely refers to the early Vimalakīrti Assembly (*Yuima-e*; 維摩会). However, while later sources such as the *Kōfukuji engi* also ascribe the origins of this elaborate ritual to Kamatari, its actual origins and early format remain unclear. In 801 Kōfukuji was designated as its permanent site. *Kōfukuji ryaku nendai ki* 興福寺略年代記, *ZGR* 29/2, 122. See also Paul Groner, *Ryōgen and Mount Hiei*, 129–130; Bauer, "The Power of Ritual," 12.

[85] Sataku Seimei (沙叱昭明; ?–?) is also mentioned in the *NS*, but there is a discrepancy regarding his rank. The *NS* states he received the 'Great Silk Cap, Lesser Rank' (大錦下) in 671, a rank lower than the one mentioned in the Kaden, seven years earlier. *TK*, 257.

[86] In the appendix to *Historiographical Trends in Early Japan*, Bentley included a translation of the Chronicle of Jōe based on a different manuscript allegedly copied in the late fourteenth century from an original owned by Kūkai. This source text is significantly different from Okimori's edited text used here. Bentley, *Historiographical Trends*, 217.

if he could not forge him how could he benefit from *Gan Jiang*?[87] Despite being as strong as an arrow, if he could not attach a bundle of feathers, how could he attain the beauty of Guiji?[88] He distanced himself from his parents' benevolence and sought the peculiarity of the high seat.[89]

In the fifth year of Hakuhō, he arrived in Chang'an, accompanying a mission to the Tang.[90] He resided at the temple of Huiri at Huaidefang where he studied under master of the Dharma Shentai.[91] This was in the fourth year of the Tang's Yong Hui era;

---

[87] The Great Minister is his father, Nakatomi/Fujiwara no Kamatari; 'benefit from *Gan Jiang*' [干将之利] refers to one member of a pair of mythical swords, the other being Mo Ye (莫耶). This reference is absent in Bentley's version. However, the mention of *Gan Jiang* confirms the extent to which the *TK* is rooted in the Chinese Classics, and is therefore of utmost importance.

[88] *Guiji* (会稽) refers to a phrase from the fourth book of the *Huainanzi*: "The beautiful things of the southeast are the arrow bamboos of Mount Guiji." Mount Guiji is one of the nine mountains mentioned earlier in the same chapter. See Liu An, *The Huainanzi*, 155 and 159.

[89] '[P]eculiarity of the high seat' [席上之珍] is taken by Okimori as referring to Confucianism, as the expression is also found in the *Li Ji*, TK, 263. However, the following sentence starts with *yue ni* (故), 'therefore,' and continues to explain that he went on to study Buddhism. For this reason, I suspect the 'high seat' here refers to a Buddhist, and not a Confucian talent.

[90] Full date: 白鳳五年歳次甲寅. *TK*, 264. I leave the calendrical sexagenary terms (*ganzhi* 干支) here and below untranslated. According to Wilkinson, there is no fixed English translation to refer to the sixty terms of the calendar and he suggests referring to the number of the dates. Wilkinson, *Chinese History, a New Manual*, p. 496. '甲寅' here refers to *jiayin* (1+ 3 in the sexagenary cycle). There is a significant discrepancy between the sources regarding the dating of his travel, life and death. As pointed out by Bingenheimer, the *Genkō shakushō* mentions the year of his departure as 653, and his return as Hakuhō 7 (678) whereas the History states he returned in Hakuhō 16 (687). Bingenheimer, *A Biographical Dictionary…*, p. 117. The *Nihon Shoki* mentions the date 653/5/12 as the date of his departure. See Aston, *Nihon shoki*, Vol. II, p. 242; NS, Hakuchi 4 (653), 5.12.

[91] Huiri (慧日; ?–748) was a well-known Tang monk and disciple of Yijing. Shentai (神泰) was a disciple of Xuanzang (玄奘; 602–664)

he was eleven years old at that time. As soon as he immersed himself in the way of the Buddha he did not waste day or night. For more than ten years he studied under his teacher. He mastered the Buddhist canon and also understood the Daoist and Confucian texts.[92] He was able to visualize poetry and observe the rules of composition.

From the ninth month, autumn, of the sixteenth year of Hakuhō, Jōe returned to the capital from Paekche.[93] He recited one line from a poem about his days in Kudara. It read:

Separated from the court by a thousand li
I gaze at autumn from the vestige of the border[94]

Closely and meticulously reading these lines, the talented of the day could not yet grasp their depth and stealthily Kudara's gentry poisoned him, jealous of his abilities. On the twenty-third day of the twelfth month of that year he passed away in his mansion in Ōhara.[95] He had twenty-three springs and autumns. The monastic and the lay shed tears, and the heart of both the court and the people was in pain.[96]

The monk Dōken from Koryŏ composed these thoughts:[97]

---

and was known for his refutation of Daoist ideas. The temple in Chang'an where he worked with Xuanzang was called *Hongfusi* (Jap.: Kōfukuji, 弘福寺). TK, 264–265.

[92] *Naikyō* (内経) or 'Buddhist canon' and *geten* (外典) or 'Daoist and Confucian texts.'

[93] Full date: 白鳳十六年歳次乙丑秋九月, TK, 267. '乙丑' refers to *yichou* (2+2) in the sexagenary cycle. Wilkinson, *Chinese History, A New Manual*, p. 496.

[94] Translated by Bingenheimer as: "Ten thousand miles away is the emperor's city, all around the city walls, autumn everywhere." See Bingenheimer, *A Biographical Dictionary*, 116.

[95] Ohara was closely connected with the Fujiwara as this might have been the birthplace of Kamatari, as mentioned in the *Tōnōmine engi*; TK, 269.

[96] 'court and people' or *chōya* (朝野).

[97] Dōken (道賢; also written as 道顕) appears in the Chronicle of Kamatari above.

When you divined our destiny, you based yourself on the former classics; when you clarified the old and the new, you used the country's eternal laws. Those who untangle the thread at the purple quarters consider it fundamental to encourage intelligence; those who bring brilliance to the sovereign's household, consider it fundamental to raise virtue. Therefore, the Duke of Zhou himself used the three rods on Bo Qin, while Kong Zi used the two teachings for Kong Li.[98] Accordingly, you provided order to the state from afar while it was clearly not your personal duty. If one contemplates this matter, in general, the courageous confront the world by establishing their reputation and glorifying their position. They exploit their abilities and discard their inabilities; there is nothing they do not know. Even more, their generosity and severity complement each other, and thus splendour and plainness transform one another. These are the achievements of holy ones. Perhaps, only you were such a man! You practiced supreme virtue, and you transcended the highest mountains. If a person would have just one of your qualities, he would already excel in virtue.

The Great Minister made you a Master of the Dharma and dispatched you to the Tang court to study.[99] You both were alike in learning and there was nothing you did not study.[100] You had the Qi Lu in your mind and the Wu Che in your chest.[101] You had insight into misfortune and fortune, and you profoundly polished your actions.[102] Gui Gu wept once again and was afraid you would separate yourself from the gentry.[103] You studied diligently.

---

[98] Bo Qin (伯禽) was the Duke of Zhou's son. Kong Li (孔鯉) was the son of Confucius. A parallel is drawn between these great figures and Kamatari and his son Jōe, undoubtedly aimed at emulating the Fujiwara patriarch's lasting legacy; *TK*, 272.

[99] 'Great Minister' is not directly expressed in the text, but I agree with Okimori that the subject of the sentence most likely is Kamatari and his son Jōe, the 'Master of the Dharma' (法師). *TK*, 275. In connection with the references to Confucius and his son above, this eulogy thus stresses the persona and the virtues of the Fujiwara patriarch.

[100] This sentence compares father and son, and then moves on to Jōe ('he').

[101] Qi Lu (七略); Wu Che (五車), both refer to compendia.

[102] 'Misfortune and fortune' (否泰) come from 否塞 and 通泰; these terms appear in the *Yijing*, *TK*, 275.

[103] The expression Gui Gu (鬼谷) refers to a teacher's tears of joy when realizing a student's progress. Here it means that the Tang court was so

The potter creates pottery and the smith forges guild objects.[104] In this manner you, knowledgeable about the arts, possessed unprecedented talent. Because of this, you instantly understood Heaven's orders, accepted the burden and ordered a palanquin.[105] Moreover, following an imperial order, Guo Wu Zong and Liu De Gao treated you lovingly from morning till evening and respectfully returned you to the Yamato court.[106] You crossed the sea route and arrived here, at the old capital.[107] His Holiness issued an order to go to his home and, happily, you accepted.[108] After having been there for some time, you rested on a sick bed and the cotton thread's movement had grown dim.[109] Ah! Why did this happen? This was on the twenty-third day of the twelfth month of Hakuhō sixteen.[110] After too few springs and autumns, you passed away at the mansion in Ōhara. Oh, how lamentable!

Following this, a death poem read:[111]

Foundation of our sovereign,
governance illumined your house.[112]
So erudite and benevolent,

---

impressed that they did not want to see him return to the Japanese court.
[104] 'He studied diligently' is a translation for the expression 韋編一絕, a term that also appears in the *Shiji*, *TK*, 276.
[105] This describes Jōe's acceptance of the role of Tang emissary.
[106] Guo Wu Zong (廓武宗) and Liu De Gao (劉德高) were both officials of the Tang court and were mentioned in the *Nihon Shoki* in entries from Tenji 3 (664) and Tenji 4 (665); *TK*, 277–278. Guo Wu Zong returned on 664/10/4 and Liu De Gao arrived at the Yamato court on 665/11/13. See, for example Aston, *Nihongi*, vol. II, p. 282 and p. 284.
[107] The 'old capital' (旧京) probably refers to the Asuka (飛鳥) palace.
[108] 'His holiness' (聖人) refers to the sovereign, here, Tenji.
[109] This expression (纊微) refers to the practice of using a thread to measure someone's breathing; *TK*, 279.
[110] Complete date: 白鳳十六年歲次乙丑十二月廿三日. 乙丑 refers to *yichou* (2+2 in the sexagenary cycle). Wilkinson, *Chinese History, a New Manual*, p. 496.
[111] The poem is comprised of fifty-five lines of four characters. I translated the verses while keeping four English words per line.
[112] The 'foundation of our sovereign' refers to Kamatari, whose qualities were passed on to his son.

wings protected our policies.[113]
Of a high repute,
promulgating the court's policies.
Oh ! Mountain. Oh! Sea,
A fortress! A wall![114]
Regulating fishing for ritual,
just like Zang Xibo.[115]
Fortune through good deeds,[116]
left to the wise.[117]

---

[113] A reference to Kamatari assisting in the application of laws and regulations under Tenji. The Chronicle of Kamatari also describes the Fujiwara patriarch as the 'wings' (翼) of the sovereign. *TK*, 282.

[114] Reference to Kamatari's moral strength.

[115] 臧僖伯; this passage refers to the official Zang Xibo who is mentioned in the *Zuozhan* as stating that living beings such as fish should not be killed unless for ritual use benefitting the state. See Roel Sterckx, *The Animal and The Daemon in Early China*, 145–146. *TK*, 283.

[116] 'Fortune through good deeds' is the translation of the concept *sekizen no yokei* (積善余慶), a phrase that is used with similar frequency in the Chronicle of Muchimaro (積善之後、余慶鬱郁), following: 'After having accumulated good deeds, his remaining virtue was maximal.' This concept also occurs in the *Nihon Shoki* in a passage referring to the year 669 when Kamatari received the name 'Fujiwara' from Tenji. The relevant passage describes how the sovereign Tenji entered Kamatari's mansion and inquired about his illness. Struck with grief, the monarch states: (my translation) 'It is no exaggeration to say that the Way of Heaven contributes to goodness, nor is it to say that, after the accumulation of good deeds, one's remaining virtue is optimal.' Aston translates: "It is surely no vain saying that the Way of Heaven helps goodness: nor is the principle that the accumulation of good actions redounds to happiness of no effect." Aston, *Nihongi*, Vol. II, p. 291. Originally occurring in the *Yijing*, this phrase refers to the transfer of morality within one's lineage through good deeds. Here, we see a clear example of how Nakamaro attempts to justify his own position through the good deeds of his forebears. See *TK*, 283; Chan, "The Kōfukuji Nan'endō and its Buddhist Icons," 87.

[117] Here, the 'wise' refers to Jōe. The focus now shifts from Kamatari to his son, but it is significant that Jōe's importance is described based on his father's character and achievements, once again connecting the narratives of both chronicles.

*Seeking the Western Tang
practicing near the Si.*[118]
*Near your master's seat,
deepening thoughts, cultivating Spirit.*[119]
*Carrying Ji Mountain's treasure,
Bian He offered advice.
Storing the jewel of the Han,
The Dragon Child passed it on to the Sui.
Welcomed at the Palace,*[120]
*raising the state's brilliance.
Receiving the court's orders,
your banner invited righteousness.
Reshaping lips and teeth,
learning through your father.*[121]
*Many imperial servants present,
The Purple Palace shines.
The Four Gates' magnificence,
the three skills thrive.*[122]
Statecraft did not weaken,

---

[118] This refers to Kong Zi instructing his disciples on the banks of the river Si (泗). Following the passages above, the Fujiwara patriarch's morality is compared with Kong Zi's character.

[119] This sentence is reminiscent of the following passage from the *The Chronicle of Kamatari*, describing the close relationship between Kamatari and his sovereign, Tenji: "When they went out they shared a carriage or rode horse side by side. Inside, their cushions touched and their knees were close." The importance of the servant is indicated by the privilege of sharing close, physical proximity to the ruler. C.f., Mikaël Bauer, "The Chronicle of Kamatari: A Short Introduction To and Translation of the First Part of the History of the Fujiwara House," 'Spirit' here refers to *shen* (神), a concept that was the subject of much speculation among several traditions.

[120] The 'palace' probably refers to the Tang court where Jōe represented the Japanese court as an emissary, but also where he was educated. He was only eleven years old upon arrival and no doubt received instruction there.

[121] 'lips and teeth' (唇齒) refers to the closeness of the Tang court and Japan; *TK*, 285. 'Your father' refers to Kamatari and once again describes the son while celebrating the Fujiwara patriarch.

[122] The 'three skills' are literary, military and oratory skills; *TK*, 286.

bolstered by the state's jewels.
Life is a plantain tree,
people pass gates, castles.[123]
Wisteria are easily cut;
four "serpents" remain unconfined![124]
Orchids shrivel in Spring,
pines wither in Summer.
The Phoenix, shot by arrows,
the bullfinch, caught in nets.
Oh! How Lamentable!
When Yan Hui was unfortunate,
Heaven was in mourning.[125]
When Ji Zi buried his son,
he expressed his vows.[126]

---

[123] The expression, 'life is a plantain tree (芭蕉)' recalls the impermanence of life. The metaphor of the plantain (banana) tree can be found in both Buddhist scriptures and later Japanese poetry. For example, in the *Vimalakīrti Sūtra*, this tree is mentioned twice: "This body is like a bubble that cannot continue for long. This body is like a flame born of longing and desire. This body is like the plantain that has no firmness in its trunk. This body is like a phantom, the product of error and confusion" (Chapter 2). Further, "[a]s the wise view the moon in the water, or a face or form seen in a mirror; as shimmers of heat in a torrid season, as the echo that follows a cry, as clouds in the sky, as foam on the water, bubbles on the water, as a thing no firmer than the trunk of the plantain, no longer lasting than a flash of lightning" (Chapter 7). See Watson, *The Vimalakirti Sutra*, 35 and 83. See also several Haiku and Noh plays where the image of the plantain tree is used to describe the fragility of the human body and life itself. For example, in Zeami's Noh play *Izutsu* (井筒) we read: "…the leaves of the plantain tree, rustling in the wind through the pines…" (松風が揺らす芭蕉の葉のうちに); for an English translation and explanation, see *Izutsu* on http://www.the-noh.com or Tyler, *Japanese Nō Dramas*, 120–132.

[124] 'Wisteria' or *sotō* (鼠藤), is equally a metaphor for the shortness of life, *TK*, 288; The "serpents" refer to the four serpents of earth, water, fire and wind; *TK*, 288.

[125] Yan Hui (顔回) was a disciple of Kong Zi. Jōe, as Kamatari's son, is compared here with Kong Zi's student.

[126] Ji Zi of Yan Ling buried his son between Ying and Bo. He is mentioned as an exemplar of propriety in the *Book of Rites* (*Liji*),

In writing you live on,
but where are your body and soul?
Seeing what you left, I think of you.
The Palace did not promote you.
Oh! How lamentable!
The cart and jewel reach Wei,
the castle's jade has left Chao.
Your talents should be cherished,
days returning, evenings fall.
Oh! How lamentable!

◻

The Chronicle of Muchimaro 武智麻呂伝

The Lower part of the History of the Fujiwara House
By the monk Enkei[127]

Muchmaro, the Fujiwara Great Minister of the Left, was a man from the Sakyō district.[128] He was the oldest son of the Head of the Council of State Fuhito, and his mother was a daughter of the Soga Great Minister of the Treasury.[129] He was born in the mansion at Ōhara on the fifteenth day of the fourth month of 680, the ninth year since the enthronement of the sovereign Tenmu.[130] Because he cultivated righteousness, he received

---

Tan Gong II, verse 196. See *Chinese Text Project*: http://ctext.org/all-texts?filter=d578

[127] 延慶 (?–?). The same monk is commonly identified as the author of the Chronicle of Jōe. Bauer, "The Chronicle of Kamatari," 207. He is also referred to as Nakamaro's 'monk in residence,' *NST*, 26. Yamagishi refers to him as a 'house monk' (家僧). See Yamagishi, *Kodai seiji*, 26.

[128] Refers to the capital's (Heijōkyō) district (左京) where Muchimaro's residence was located.

[129] Fuhito is referred to by the character 史; Yamagishi, *Kodai seiji*, 26, see also *TK*, 291–292. The 'Soga Great Minister of the Treasury' (蘇我蔵大臣) might refer to the grandson of Soga no Umako.

[130] 天武天皇即位九年歳庚辰. Kamatari is also said to have been born here, *NST*, 22. '庚辰' refers to *genchen* (7+5 in the sexagenary cycle). Wilkinson, *Chinese History, A New Manual*, p. 496.

this name.¹³¹ When he was still a young child, he mourned the loss of his mother. He wept tears of blood and broke down. He took nothing by mouth, and his health declined. From then on his condition was weak and although he made the effort to continue, he was of a poor constitution ever since.

As years went by, he did not associate himself with trivial matters.¹³² His appearance was tall; his speech heavy and slow. His character was warm and good, and his heart was sincere and steadfast. What was not respectful, he did not adopt; what was not righteous, he did not request.¹³³ He always preferred neutrality; from afar he shunned conflict. One time, he played Go while the day passed; another time, he was reading all night. He did not love wealth or sensuality; he never manifested either happiness or anger.¹³⁴ He valued honor and faith and acted out of compassion and righteousness.¹³⁵ When someone praised him, he never replied; when someone slighted him, he never engaged.

He was honest and did not tolerate dishonesty, he was incorruptible and did not tolerate corruption. He fully comprehended the significance of the hundred scholars and the meaning of the Three Profound Teachings.¹³⁶

He especially valued the teachings of Śākyamuni and combined these with Daoist practices.¹³⁷ He honoured those who

---

[131] The character 茂 can be read as 'moshi' which inspired the 'muchi' of his name 'Muchimaro'; see also *TK*, 295. 'Muchi' means 'noble,' *NST*, 26.

[132] The word used for 'trivial matters' is 小節 and refers to those matters not associated with righteousness (義) or principle (理). The word appears in several Chinese sources used throughout the *Tōshi Kaden*, such as the *Shiji*, NST, 26; Yamagishi, *Kodai seiji*, 26.

[133] Yamagishi points out that this statement is paraphrased from the *Yijing*; see also *TK*, 298.

[134] Wealth or sensuality refers to the compound 財色; *TK*, 298.

[135] Bohner translates 信 as 'Vertrauen' (trust) but adds 'Glauben' (faith) as an alternative interpretation. Bohner, "Muchimaro-Den," 420. Benevolence (仁) and Righteousness (義).

[136] 'the hundred scholars' (百家) refers to 'the teachings of many scholars,' *NST*, 26. *TK*, 299. 'The Three Profound Teachings' (三玄) are the *Zhuangzi* (莊子), the *Laozi* (老子), and the *Yijing*.

[137] 'Daoist practices' is the translation of the term *bukuni* 服餌, which refers to a type of medicine aimed at immortality; see also Yamagishi, *Kodai seiji*, 27; *TK*, 299.

followed the Way and he respected those who displayed virtue.[138] He respected hardship and poverty, and felt compassion for the orphaned and the lonely. Each year in the third month of summer, he invited ten Great Virtuous Ones and listened to their commentary on the flower of the Dharma.[139] This permeated his soul. To him, admonishing the higher classes was as abhorrent as pulling off his own clothes. Because his mansion was located to the south of the palace he was commonly called the Southern Courtier.[140]

One time, when he was young, Imperial Prince Hozumi met him at a banquet.[141] The prince reflected on the past and said to the assembled nobles:

> Often I see children of the Fujiwara family. This child is of exceptional talent and differs from other people. I heard that 'the cubs of tigers and leopards, although not yet full grown, have the will to devour sheep. The chicks of geese and cranes, despite their wings not yet fully grown, have the will to fly across the four seas.'[142] This child will certainly attain the rank of the Ting cauldron.[143]

In the first year of Taihō, the children of good families were selected to become chamberlains.[144] As child of the three

---

[138] The *Liji* (礼記) refers to prior rulers as respecting both the Way (道) and Virtue (徳). *TK*, 299.

[139] This 'Flower of the Dharma' (法花) is a reference to the Lotus Sutra (*Hokke kyō* 法華経). Possibly this refers to the Hokke-e at Kōfukuji, though it is not clear whether or in what capacity this ritual existed at this temple.

[140] For example, the *Shoku Nihongi* refers to him as the 'southern courtier' (南卿) at times. *TK*, 300. His branch was therefore referred to also as the 'Southern House' of the Fujiwara.

[141] Imperial Prince Hozumi 穂積親王 (?–715) was the fifth son of Tenmu.

[142] The 'Four Seas' (四海), signifying all under Heaven (天下).

[143] Meaning he will certainly attain a high bureaucratic rank.

[144] 'Good families' refers here to the noble class of the *ryōke* (良家). Chamberlain refers to *udoneri* (舎人). Taiho 1 (大宝元年) or 701. The *Shoku Nihongi* refers to this event, showing that children of the higher nobility followed a different, faster route to bureaucratic positions, *TK*, 304. The position of *udoneri* fell under the office of

highest ranks he was ordered to be promoted to the sixth rank, and he was made chamberlain. He was twenty-two. An imperial rescript stated:

> Your house illuminates the imperial household and your service to the sovereign is well documented. Your current rank does not sufficiently celebrate you. The issuing of the new legal codes has brought order to the country and to its people.[145] Because of its requirements, this rank has now been conferred upon you.

The official of the Great Minister's house Oharida no Shibi was dissatisfied and spoke:[146]
Ah! Why does this household's heir hold this low rank?
His heart was troubled and his face reddened with shame. Someone informed the Great Minister, who ordered his household:

> The state has institutionalized new legal codes. So, according to precedent, the rank has been conferred on this boy. Why be ashamed? Moreover, stop your slander!

As Chamberlain, Muchimaro could go in and out the palace. Those who saw him rejoiced in his good morality, those who associated with him responded to his mildness and refinement. His contemporaries spoke among themselves and stated: 'People should be like the Great Minister's eldest son.'

Nakatsukasa shō (中務省) and became part of an elite track called on'i (陰位); it is uncertain from what year exactly this system existed. Kimoto, *Fujiwara no Nakamaro: sossei*, 7.

[145] This refers to the promulgation of the *Taihō ritsuryō*. However, these weren't put into effect until 757 by Nakamaro. It is not a coincidence that these codes are mentioned in reference to Fuhito since this passage draws once again a clear link between Nakamaro and the name of his grandfather.

[146] 'Great Minister' (大臣) refers to Fujiwara no Fuhito. Oharida no Shibi (?–?; 小治田志毘) does not appear anywhere else but Okimori mentions that it might be connected with a family that lived at an area called Oharida located in Yamato. *TK*, 305.

In the first month of the second year he was promoted to the Ministry of Justice.[147] He attended to his bureaucratic position and thoroughly understood its matters. He was just and not selfish. He assessed people's words and carefully considered their expressions.[148] Never did he miss their intentions. When deciding a doubtful case, he justified the verdict with prudence. Although there were great and small cases to be handled, his office did not have an established procedure. Legal documents were chaotic, and judgment was not just.

Thereupon he recorded the preceding and aftermath of judgments as legal articles and presented these to the court. Before the first year of the Taihō era these were not yet ratified, but afterwards they became part of the legal corpus. From then on plaintiffs settled their matters internally and no longer presented their case to the court. In the fourth month of the third year he became ill and withdrew.

In the third month of the fourth year Muchimaro became vice-head of the Academy.[149] In previous years, following the demise of the Kiyomihara sovereign, the state flourished and the people carried out their duties. In addition, the sovereign's cart had moved to the capital Fujiwara-kyō and since all were occupied no one wanted to study at the time.[150] Therefore the Academy had fallen in decline, and the students were scattered. Although the Academy existed, it seemed that nothing was happening there.

When he entered the Academy, and saw it empty and deserted, he thought: "This Academy is a place where wisdom and talent congregate, a place where the sovereign's influence is valued.

---

[147] Taihō 2 or 702. 'Ministry of Justice' refers to the Kyōbushō (刑部省). Bohner translated this as Muchimaro becoming a 'judge' (Richter), Bohner, "Muchimaro-Den," 423.

[148] This is a direct paraphrasing of a passage of the *Lun yu*: '察言而觀色.' The question raised in the analects pertains to the qualities of a distinguished official. *Lun yu* 12.20. Muchimaro is described in the same terms as the ideals described in this passage: not 'notoriety' (聞) but 'righteousness' (義) determined the quality of the official.

[149] The 'Daigaku no suke' (大学助).

[150] 'Kiyomihara sovereign' (浄御原天皇) refers to Tenmu's passing in 686.

It rectifies the state, rectifies the households, and all depend upon its holy teachings. However, loyalty has withered, and filial piety has withered. We have distanced ourselves from the Way. Now, those who study are few, and the wind of *Ru* does not blow.[151] This is not how one evokes the sacred Way, or supports the authority of the sovereign."

Along with the High Official Prince Rōgu, Muchimaro began to invite scholars; the Classics and Histories were debated and explained.[152] Within twelve days the school flourished, and students from near and far gathered like the clouds and aligned like the stars. The sound of recitation was heard everywhere.

In the second year of the Keiun era, during the mid-spring Sekiten, Muchimaro said to the Ru scholar Tori Yasutsugu:[153]

> We have learned through transmission that 'If for three years there are no rites, then the rites will surely fade away. If for three years there is no music, the music will surely perish.' Now, the day of the Sekiten has become obscure. I request to write a text to celebrate the spirits of our prior teachers, to pass them down to inform the customs of future generations.

And so Yasutsugu wrote a text on the Sekiten. The verses said:

> On a given day, month and year, we, the families of the bureau of the Academy, respectfully celebrate the spirit of the

---

[151] Ru (儒) refers to the correct application of ritual or the ritual organization of the state.

[152] High Official or *chōkan / kami* (長官); Rōgu 良虞 (?-737) was from Paekche descent. The *SN* mentions his death in the seventh month of Tenpyō 9 (737).

[153] Tori Yasutsugu 刀利康嗣; The Sekiten (Ch.: *shidian*; 釈奠). The first mention of this ritual dates back to 701/2/14, as recorded in the *Shoku Nihongi*. Ian James McMullen has pointed out the significance of this ritual being included in the section of the *gakuryō* (administrative ordinances for schools), rather than under the *Jingikan* (神祇官). McMullen also states that Muchimaro 'rescued the university from the decline into which it had apparently fallen' and refers to *Muchimaro den* translated here: I.J. McMullen, "The Worship of Confucius in Ancient Japan,", 50–54.

Minister of Justice Lu Kung Hsuan-Fu with clear alcohol and sacrificial food.[154] Brilliantly you descend from Mount Ni and celebrate.[155] Here, as leader and saint, you embody the extraordinary form of a thousand years, and you respond to the bad fate of a hundred kings. When the lord is lowly, there is rebellion. Rites cease and music is destroyed. Lamenting the fall of the Zhou, you returned to Qi having left Lu. Chen faced misfortune and Kuang was encircled. Xia Cai experienced pain. You had three thousand students, of them seventy were capable. You spread loyalty and piety from Si Shui, and investigated the virtue and righteousness of Tang Yao and Yu Shun. The verses of the Classic of Poetry all found their proper place, and robes and caps were awarded correctly.[156]

Why does one say it is difficult to contain crumbling mountains, and why were the songs of the Liang recited so quickly?[157] Water does not stop flowing, and rituals were organized between the two pillars.[158] Oh! How moving! Now, the holy court is grand, and the School is vast. The fragrant virtue is praised and acclaimed, the highest way is contemplated and admired. If there is a soul or a spirit it will transform and head to this feast.[159]

---

[154] Bureau of the Academy refers to the *daigaku ryō* (大学寮). 'On a given day, month and year' specifically refers to 某年月日朔丁. 'Minister of Justice' refers to the title 司寇, a Zhou period office. *TK*, 317.

[155] Bohner translates this as 'Mount Gen Ni' (Gen Ni-shan). See Bohner, "Muchimaro-Den," 423.

[156] A paraphrase of 雅頌各得其所 taken from the *Lun yu* 9.15.

[157] 'The songs of the Liang' (梁歌) might refer to a passage from the *Liji*, *TK*, 319.

[158] 'The flow of the water does not stop' refers to a passage from the *Lun yu*: 子在川上曰逝者如斯夫不舍晝夜. The image of the flowing stream can also be found in later Japanese literature, the most famous example being undoubtedly Kamo no Chōmei's classical Japanese phrase　ゆく河の流れは絶えずして、しかももとの水にあらず 'the flow of the river is never cut, yet its water never remains the same.' The 'offerings between the two pillars' is a reference to a passage from the *Liji*: 予疇昔之夜，夢坐奠於兩楹之間 'last night I dreamt that I was sitting with the offerings to the dead by my side between the two pillars ' (trans. James Legge, ctext.org).

[159] 'Soul' or *shen* (神).

In the twelfth month of that year, he was promoted to the fifth lower rank. At that time he was twenty-six. In the seventh month of the third year, he transferred and became Head of the Academy.[160] He frequently entered the school building, assembled the students of Ru and recited the Book of Odes and the Book of History, and he unrolled and perused the Book of Rites and the Book of Changes. He enforced and praised the school, and guided its students. The students of literature all applied themselves to their work.

In the third month of the first year of the Wadō era, he was promoted to Head of the Library which he combined with the position of Chamberlain.[161] He served at the Inner Palace at court and discretely received the commands of the sovereign. At that time he catalogued the archives of the library. Previously, following the disturbances and turmoil of the Jinshin years, the scrolls of the bureaucratic texts had been either scattered around or parts of the cases had been lost.[162]

He appealed to the throne to call upon the people to look for copies to reconstruct the lost sources. Through these efforts, these bureaucratic texts were largely restored. As a bureaucrat he was diligent and therefore he did not slow down, nor did he rest. Because he embodied benevolence he was able to lead men. Because he was pure and strong he was able to handle matters skillfully. For this reason, he was promoted to the Vice Fifth Upper Rank in the fourth month.[163]

In the sixth month of the fifth year, he was appointed governor of Ōmi province. Ōmi province is a famous land under heaven. Its territory is vast and its people are many, the province is wealthy and its families are prosperous. To the East it intersects with the Fuha region, to the North it borders Tsuruga. When one passes through

---

[160] Head of the Academy refers to *daigaku no kami* (大学頭).

[161] 'Chamberlain' refers to *jiju* (侍従); Wadō 1 (和銅元年) or 708, indicating the reign of Genmei 元明天皇 (707–715).

[162] The Jinshin (壬申) rebellion of 672 following a succession dispute after Tenji. The first part of the *History of the Fujiwara House*, the *Chronicle of Kamatari*, includes a passage in which Kamatari prevents further violence after the future Tenmu throws a spear into the floor during a banquet at Ōtsu.

[163] Vice Fifth Upper Rank or 従五位上.

Yamashiro in the South one arrives at the capital.[164] Its water and sea are clear and vast, its mountains and trees are thick and high. Its soil is dark and its fields are of the best quality. Despite the danger of flooding, since ancient times there hasn't been worry that wasn't surmounted. This is why holy lords and wise servants had moved the capital to Ōmi. The young and the old jointly acted in accordance with Heaven, going around holding hands, dancing and singing on the wide roads.[165] At the time, people said it was an era of great peace. This road of public and private traffic became the gateway to the Eastern and Western areas. If governing takes place in haste, then people loudly claim falsehood and flee afar; if governing is loose, then people look down upon authority and violate the land. He guided the people virtuously, and harmonized the people through rites.[166] Pardoning small offences, he initiated change; carrying out rule through contemplation, he listened to the masses. He entered the villages, respectfully visited the fathers and elders, understood the hardships of common people and changed the evil policies of the state. He promoted agriculture and the cultivation of mulberry fields. The people were employed during the working seasons.[167] When it was time for corvée, he put the rich and those who had many healthy servants first, and the poor and those who only had the weak to help, second.

He respected the elders and felt compassion for the young, allowing them to have their own belongings. The people of the country rejoiced:

When the noble one nears the border, the people feel restored.

In general, he was respected and all looked up to him.

---

[164] The capital (京) here is Heijō-kyō.
[165] 'acted in accordance with Heaven' is in this instance the translation for *wuwei* 無為.
[166] This passage appears in the *Lunyu* 2.3 道之以德，齊之以禮，有恥且格. The consequence is that a people led through virtue and rites, will ultimately become good, in contrast to a people led by law and punishment.
[167] Refers to the phrase in the *Lunyu* 1.5 使民以時, 'to employ the people during the proper seasons'.

In the first month of the sixth year, he was promoted to Vice Fourth Lower Rank.[168] At the time he was thirty-four years old. From a young age he respected and valued the Three Jewels, and eagerly listened to the Marvellous Law.[169] He wished to find the fruit of the Buddhist teachings, and even when finishing his meal he could not forget about it. Despite having civil duties, he always prayed at a site of worship. Once he unexpectedly entered a temple, and inside it was cold and everything was in disarray.[170] The halls and shrines were falling down and collapsing, the monks' quarters and hallways were empty and quiet. He turned to the people of the area, asking them about it and they replied:

> The temple's donor fully controlled the temple's possessions and land, and did not allow the monks and nuns to be custodians or to use it freely. This is why the temple is in disarray and damaged. And not just this temple, all the others as well.

Muchimaro spoke:

> The Thus Come One appeared in the world, preached the entire Dharma and brought peace to suffering living beings. Thus, he brought about the root for good karma.[171] His teaching was deep and marvelous, and from the land of Tenjiku changed Shintan and reached these lands.[172] Those who understand the gate of the Dharma separate themselves from afflictions, those who lose the way of the Dharma turn the wheel of life and death.[173] How can white-clad donors thoughtlessly

---

[168] *SN* Wadō 6 (713). 1. 23; *TK*, 331.

[169] Marvelous Law or *myōhō* 妙法), referring to the teachings of the Lotus Sutra, the *Hokke kyō* 法華経.

[170] 'Temple' or *dera* (寺) designating perhaps an official temple, in contrast to the 'site of worship' (精舎). The latter could also be translated as 'temple' but the former is an official category.

[171] The 'Thus Come One' (*nyorai* 如来) refers to the historical Buddha. '...brought peace to suffering living beings' is implied in the term *kyōke* 教化.

[172] *Tenjiku* (天竺) and *Shintan* (震檀) refer to India and China.

[173] 'Afflictions' or *gaiten* (蓋纏) that prevent one from gaining insight.

administer the affairs of monks,[174] not providing for the clergy and neglecting the temple?[175] This does not benefit the state's field of merit and results in bad karma, harming living beings.[176]

Following Muchimaro offered a memorial to the throne:[177]

> Your servant, luckily immersed in the Great Change, is the protector of one province.[178] Because of his public duties he moves amongst the people and in his own time he went to pray at a site of worship. The people of the region do not understand cause and result, and the descendants of the lay patrons, not paying attention to bad karma, administered monastic affairs while solely devoting themselves to raising their families. The monks and nuns enter fictitious names in the temple registrars, are dispersed and live in the villages. It was never anyone's intention to destroy this historic temple, but it has reached the point where cows and horses trample and ruin it. This is not how the state regulates monks and nuns; this is not how people are converted to Buddhism.[179] If we do not act, the Righteous Law might fall into decline. I humbly request a clear judgement.

An edict was issued:[180]

> The worship and celebration of the Treasury of the Dharma has respect as its basis. Practice at Buddhist sites, has purity as its foremost concern. Now I have heard that the temples of the country are not being run in accordance with the law. When a thatched temple opens for the first time, it should be thus: the building is purified and the records are kept, banners are donated and following land is requested. If not, if the

---

[174] 'White clad' or *byaku e* (白衣) refers to the lay (in contrast with the monastic) patrons.
[175] 'Clergy' or *hōryo* (法侶).
[176] 'Field of merit' or *fukuden* (福田), a reference to the three treasures (*sanbō* 三宝) mentioned above.
[177] The *Shoku Nihongi* included such a memorial from the fifth month of 716 (Reiki 2), in which Muchimaro addresses Genshō.
[178] 'Great Change' or taika (大化).
[179] 'converted to Buddhism' or *butsuke* (仏化).
[180] See also the *Shoku Nihongi* for the 5th month of Reiki 2 (716).

buildings are not kept, then cows and horses trample and ruin it, the gardens are overgrown and deserted, and thorns grow freely. Subsequently, the unparalleled image of the Buddha is eternally covered with dust and the immensely profound storehouse of the Dharma is exposed to wind and rain. Generations pass and the temples fall into decline without being restored. If one explains by merely pointing out these matters, it falls short of respectful conduct. Therefore, in several areas a number of temples should be combined and consolidated. We desire they combine their forces to restore the splendour of the declined Dharma. I clearly appeal to the National Lecturer: the monks and the lay patrons should provide a list of workings of the temple, its profits and possessions. They should include this in a memorandum to the throne and then wait for proceedings."[181] Hereafter, the people of the province refrained from committing their crimes, and no longer continued to use the temple's possessions. Can we see in this Confucius' message: 'The virtue of one's Lord is like the wind?[182]

When Muchimaro went to the district of Sakata to inspect whether the order was followed, he said, gazing at Yamagawa:

I desire to climb mount Ibuki and worship.[183]

---

[181] The 'National Lecturer' refers to the position of *kokushi* (国師).
[182] Reference to the *Lun yu* 12.19: 君子之德風，小人之德草。草上之風，必偃．"The virtue of the junzi is the wind, the virtue of the commoner is the grass. When the wind blows over the grass, the grass will surely bend." (own translation)
[183] It is possible that this concerns an instance of 'gazing over the country' (*kunimi*, 国見), a ritual during which the authority of the sovereign over the country was confirmed. See also *TK*, 34. Ebersole ascribes three characteristics to this type of ritual. First, it involves a sovereign or ritual functionary to ascend a mountain. It is clear that the Fujiwara, through their Nakatomi ancestry, had a strong connection with ritual function. Second, the sovereign or official surveys/ gazes at the country. The passage here describes how Muchimaro wanders the site. Third, word of praise and awe are uttered, celebrating the landscape in which they wander. Ebersole, *Ritual Poetry*, 23–25. While no actual *kunimi uta* appears to be included here (as can be found in the *Man'yōshu* for example), the passage as a whole could

The people of the region said:

> If you enter this mountain, gales, thunder and rain will follow. Clouds and mist will blind all in obscurity, and swarms of wasps will fly up. In the past, Prince Yamato Takeru soothed the evil demons and spirits of the Eastern lands and when he returned to this world he climbed the mountain. When he had climbed half way up, he was harmed by the gods, changed into a white bird and flew into the sky.

Muchimaro said:

> For my whole life, I have never neglected demons and spirits. If they possess knowledge, then why would they harm me? If they do not possess knowledge, then how can they quietly harm people?

Thereupon, he cleansed himself and started climbing at twilight with five or six men. While they were walking, close to the summit, suddenly two wasps flew towards Muchimaro, threatening to sting him. He raised his sleeves and whipped them off, with a commanding hand. The wasps ceased and flew off. All those who followed him said:

> His virtuous conduct touches the gods and thus he shall not be harmed.

Till the day ended they wandered about in good spirits, and they walked around and worshipped. The wind and the rain quieted down simultaneously and the skies cleared up. This was the result of his powers. Afterwards, during his own free time, he went to a mountain temple in Shiga. He paid his respects to the central image of worship and aroused his intention to attain enlightenment.[184]

---

be identified as an instance of 'gazing over the country,' affirming the unbreakable link between the sovereign and the Fujiwara, the main purpose of the History of the Fujiwara House as a whole.

[184] 発願 (*hotsugan*) is here translated as 'to arouse the aspiration to attain enlightenment.'

He cut his attachment to body and mind and repented his sins. He received the precepts, purified himself, and fasted.[185] He had a divine sword made and presented it to the throne through an emissary. The emperor greatly rejoiced and issued an imperial edict:[186]

> I have heard that 'the sword is the virtuous man's military preparation to protect the body.'[187] Lately our movement and rest are unsettled and it seems our soul is lost. When I take this divine sword, the drowsiness of the night settles completely. Truly, the divine sword given by Muchimaro, the governor of Ōmi province, is a symbol of the protection of the body. Wise men of the past said: 'There is no virtue that is not announced, no word that is not rewarded.' Ten chō will be given as reward for this sign of loyalty.

Muchimaro conducted policy for the greater good and day by day rejoicing voices were added. Therefore, in the first month of the eight year he was promoted to the vice fourth upper rank.[188] Thereupon, he cut down the amount of corvée in the country and the people had more free time. He respected the way of non-acting and comprehended the false and the arcane.[189] He wandered around gracefully and satisfied, and entrusted his mind to the unseen. Following, he climbed Mount Hiei, and stayed there while the days passed. There, he planted a Yanagi tree and spoke to those who had followed him:

> Ah! You, inform those who will come after us about how we wandered and how we breathed.

---

[185] It is not clear what is meant with 'he received the precepts' (受戒), since it cannot be verified that Muchimaro ever received the precepts or was included into a particular lineage.

[186] Edict or *mikotonori* (勅).

[187] This is a quotation from the *Han shu*, TK, 346.

[188] 和銅八年 or 715. This is also mentioned in the *Shoku Nihongi* in the first month of Wadō 8. TK, 349.

[189] Refers to the arcane, unseen essence that underlies phenomena.

In that year, people from the capital's left district caught an auspicious turtle and the eighth year of the Wadō era became the first year of Reiki. In the past, the minister had met a strange man in a dream. His looks were unusual and he said:

> Men and gods both know you adore and yearn for the law of the Buddha.[190] Please construct a temple for me and help to fulfill my vow. Because of past karma, I became a god quite a long time ago.[191] Now I wish to return to the way of the Buddha and perform meritorious deeds, but I have not yet been able to understand all karmic causes and conditions.[192] Therefore I have come and made this announcement.

Muchimaro wondered whether this was Kehi no Kami but woke up from the dream before he could reply. Thereupon he prayed to the deity:

> The ways of men and gods are different, the hidden and the apparent are not the same. Who was the strange man of my dream last night? Who was he? If the god reveals a sign, I will surely build a temple!

Then, the god revealed the sign Muchimaro wanted: he picked up Ubasoku Kume Katsutari and placed him at the top of a high tree. Now knowing the reality of his dream, Muchimaro built a temple. The shrine-temple now located in Koshinomichi province is in fact this holy site.[193]

---

[190] Richard Bowring refers to unpublished work by Weinstein in his discussion of this passage, one of the earliest examples of how local deities came to be worshipped at Buddhist temples. Bowring, *The Religious Traditions of Japan*, 94.

[191] Bowring, quoting Weinstein, includes the translation 'Because of my past actions, I became a deity a long time ago.' Bowring, *The Religious Traditions of Japan*, p. 94. 'Past actions' or ' Past karma' here refers to *shukugō*. Tsuji Zennosuke, in his *Nihon bukkyōshi*, also refers to this very passage when discussing the merging of Buddhism and kami worship. Tsuji, *Nihon bukkyōshi*, vol. I, 439–441.

[192] A reference to the concept of *innen* (因縁), 'causes and conditions.'

[193] 'shrine temple' here refers to *jingūji* (神宮寺); *TK*, 354.

In the tenth month of the second year of Reiki, he was promoted to senior official of ceremonial affairs.[194] In the ninth month of Yōrō 2, he became the minister of ceremonial affairs.[195] The ministry of ceremonial affairs oversees the state's evaluations of officials and the bestowal of ranks, for all of the court officials and the hundred bureaus.[196] The strength of the public official involved justice for the public, and the bestowal of ranks was arranged and managed through the evaluation of achievement and ability. He understood the intricate standards of the high and the low, and, through praise or negative evaluation, people would be adjudicated for promotion. From that moment on, the state's evaluations were purged of all falsehood and abuse of power.

In the first month of the third year, he proceeded to Lower Fourth Rank.[197]

At that time, Mōke no kimi had his coming of age ceremony; his disposition looked very good.[198] The weight of being a master and teacher renders a person beautiful. Then, in the seventh month, he was appointed mentor of the Crown Prince. He went in and out the Spring Palace, and assisted the Crown Prince, advancing his study of literature to rectify him with established tradition. The Crown Prince gave up hunting and dedicated himself to the good karma of studying literature. Because of this, after the enthronement, he always conducted good policy, showed compassion towards the people, and worshiped and valued the Buddhist Law.

In the first month of the fifth year, Muchimaro proceeded to Vice Third Rank and was promoted to Middle Counsellor.[199] In the ninth month, he combined this with Minister of Construction of the Palace. At the time, he was forty-two years old. He directed the construction workers, planned and constructed the inner palace, restored

---

[194] Reiki 2 or 716.
[195] 'The second year of Yōrō' or 718. Reference to the title of *shikibukyō* (式部卿).
[196] *tenka* (天下) or 'state'.
[197] 正四位下
[198] Mōke no kimi (儲后) is the later sovereign Shōmu, who was the son of Fujiwara no Fuhito's daughter Fujiwara no Miyako 藤原宮子 (?–754). In other words, Muchimaro was Mōke no kimi's direct uncle.
[199] Middle Counselor or *chūnagon* (中納言).

and renovated the old structure. The palace became abundantly beautiful and people revered the sovereign. In the second month of the first year of Shinki, he proceeded to the Third Rank and oversaw the construction of the palace as before.[200] In the seventh month of the fifth year, he was appointed protector of Harima, which he combined with the position of Royal Inspector.[201]

In the sixth year he was promoted to Senior Counsellor on the Council of State.[202] He was mild and refined, and prepared for all matters. Consequently he was the throat and tongue to support the way of the king.[203] He accompanied the imperial palanquin; when they entered he held the central pole. When the court was assembled, he maintained sincerity and remained in harmony. At court, the high and the low were peaceful and quiet, and in the state there was no hatred and pain.

At that time, Imperial Prince Toneri was the liaison between the throne and the Council of State, and Imperial Prince Niitabe was in charge of all general bureaucratic matters.[204] His younger brother, the Northern Noble, was in charge of the central matters.[205] The high nobles advising on the Council of State were Middle Counselor Tachihi no Agatamori, his third younger brother and official of rites Umakahi, his fourth younger brother and official of military matters Maro, official of the large repository Prince Suzuka, and Controller of the Left Prince Katsuraki.[206] The refined chamberlains were Prince Mutobe, Prince Nagata, Prince Kadobe, Prince Sai, Prince Sakurai, Ishikawa no Ason Kimiko, Abe no Ason Yasumaro, Okisome no Takumi and others,

---

[200] 神亀元年 or 724.
[201] 神亀五年 or 728.
[202] Muchimaro becomes here Dainagon (大納言) on the Daijōkan (Council of State).
[203] To be the 'throat and tongue' of the sovereign is an expression found in several Chinese texts. For example, in the *Shijing*: 出納土命、王之喉舌。賦政于外、四方爰發; *Be the king's throat and tongue; Spread his government abroad, So that in all quarters it shall be responded to*. Trans. James Legge, ctext.org.
[204] Prince Toneri (舎人親王) was Tenmu's third son; Prince Niitabe (新田部親王) was the seventh son of Tenmu, *TK*, 367.
[205] This refers to Muchimaro's younger brother Fujiwara no Fusasaki.
[206] The 'advisors on the Council of State' refers to the *sangi* (参議).

in total more than ten people.[207] The Confucian scholars were Moribe no Muraji Ōsumi, Ochi no Atahi Hiroe, Seuna no Kōbun, Yatsume no Sukune Mushimaro, Shioya no Muraji Emaro, Narahara no Miyatsuko Azumahito, and others.[208] The literati were Ki no Ason Kiyobito, Yamada no Fubito Mikata, Fujii no Muraji Hironari, Takaoka no Muraji Kawachi, Kudara no Kimi Yamatomaro, Ōyamato no Ikimio Azumahito. The geomants were Kichita no Muraji Yoroshi, Mitachi no Muraji Gomyō, Kinoe no Muraji Matate, Chōfukushi and others. The Yin-Yang specialists were Tsumori no Muraji Tōru, Yo no Ma Hito, Ō no Chūmon, Ōtsu nu Muraji Obito, Kokuna Kōju and others.[209] Those who calculate the calendar were Yamaguchi no Imikitanushi, Shiki no Muraji Ōji, Kisakibe no Iwamura, Shii Muraji Mitasuki and others. The masters of spells were Yononinkun and Karakuni no Muraji Hirotari. In the Ministry of Monastic Affairs were Shōsōzu Jin'e and Master of Precepts Dōji.[210]

The state thrived and prospered, and the storehouses were abundant and overflowing. All under Heaven was in Great Peace. On the street, quarters shone in vermillion and purple splendour, and saddled horses lined the streets. The prisons were few and deserted. On the stones of happiness, moss flourished. Accordingly, Muchimaro embellished the capital and all postal stations; he allowed people to build tiled houses and abundantly adorn with red and white. When spring and autumn arrived, he used to assemble a literary gathering of the men of letters and talent in Suge to accrue good merit. Scholars of the time competed to win a seat at this event. This was called 'the tallying of points at the dragon's gate.'

In the ninth month of the third year of the Tenpyō era, Muchimaro was appointed official of Dazaifu in Tsukushi. Tsukushi was of strategic importance for the state. Located at the coast, it was a headquarters to defend against piracy. He protected the state's large network and he generally conducted gentle rule. Despite himself having been in the imperial palace, the people's desires for him were simi-

---

[207] 'Chamberlains' or *jijū* (侍従).
[208] 'Confucian scholars' or *shukuju* (宿儒).
[209] 'Yin-Yang specialists' here refers to *onmyō* (陰陽).
[210] 'Master of Precepts' or *risshi* (律師).

lar to those of an arrived guest. Therefore, the sovereign's spring and autumn greatly flourished, and the matters of state were not neglected. In his heart there was benevolence and love, and through his intentions he conducted good rule. There had not yet been a man like this in the position of Great Minister. Because his actions were prepared and highly composed, and because he was able to correctly follow the regulations, he was promoted to second rank to become Grand Minister of the Right. That year was the sixth year of the Tenpyō era and he was fifty-five years old.[211]

He was involved in evaluations and laboured tirelessly till the end of each day. He pacified the state and consoled the people. Despite his rank and position being respected, he had integrity and became increasingly modest. He divided his possessions at home and he assembled and protected the poor and the lonely; he dispensed thread and cotton and always donated to the Three Jewels. He frequently reflected upon the court's policies, and always worried about deficiencies in policy. In matters of state, there was nothing that he knew of and had not acted upon; in matters of compassionate requests, there was nothing he had heard of and had not granted. Based on this, calamities under heaven steadily declined, and the demons and gods did not retaliate. The people's households were adequate, and the court appeased the state through not acting.[212]

In the seventh month of the ninth year, he fell ill and increasingly stayed at home; the court lamented this. On the twenty-fourth day, the imperial consort herself went to him and issued a decree inquiring about his illness.[213] He was promoted to the second rank and proceeded to the position of Grand Minister of the Left. The following day he passed away at his private residence in the left district of the capital. He was fifty-eight springs and autumns. When the sovereign heard of his death, he felt unceasing sorrow in his chest. The court halted for three days.

---

[211] 天平六年 or 734.
[212] 'non acting' or *wuwei*. The sentence 'The people's households were sufficient' (百姓家給人足) is literally taken from the Huainanzi: " Lord Millet thus taught them how to break the earth and clear the plants, fertilize the soil, and plant the grain, giving the households sufficiency" Adapted from Liu An, *The Huainanzi*, 727.
[213] 'Consort' or *kōgō* (皇后), here Kōmyō (光明皇后; 701–760).

Musicians beating drums and playing flutes followed his corpse, draped in feathers. On the fifth day of the eight month, Muchimaro was cremated on the Saho mountain and rites were held.

 His legitimate wife was a grandchild of Grand Minister Abe on her mother's side. She raised two sons. The oldest one was Toyonari and the younger one Nakamaro. They studied under scholars, and silk garments were often offered to soften the labor of their teachers. Having talent for study, both sons' good reputation spread to the people. Toyonari achieved the position of Great Minister of the Left and as rank he reached the Second Rank. Later, when he did not report an anomaly to the throne and did not do anything about it, he was demoted to governor in Dazaifu.[214] Nakamaro had his name changed into 'Oshikatsu'.[215] Through appointment he reached the position of Daishi and he entered second rank.[216] As feathers and wings of the sovereign he gently stroked all under heaven. A eulogy states:

> After having accumulated good deeds, his remaining virtue was utmost.[217] All caps succeed each other, supporting the imperial cart, across several generations they have become the sovereign's ears and eyes. Heaven above is in peace and the state below is prosperous. Demons and gods are close and in harmony. The state and the family were joint together. Esteemed because of his loyalty and devotion, this man was like a gem.

---

[214] *Ingai no sochi* (員外師).

[215] Oshikatsu 押勝. This is confirmed in Nakamaro's eulogy in the *Shoku Nihongi*

[216] He received the rank on Tenpyō Hōji 4 (760).1.4. The edict compares Nakamaro (referred to as *Fujiwara Emi no Asomi* 藤原恵美朝臣 to his grandfather Fuhito (and thus not to his own father, Muchimaro). Bender, *The Edicts*, 83–84.

[217] 'After having accumulated good deeds, his remaining virtue was utmost' refers to the concept *sekizen no yokei* (積善余慶) also mentioned in the Chronicle of Jōe above. The second occurrence of this concept in the third and final chronicle seems to confirm the connection between these biographies. Yamagishi mentions that this line confirms the transfer of good merit from the patriarch to his descendants. Yamagishi, *Kodai seiji*, 38.

Bibliography

⌘

Primary sources

DNBZ *Dai Nihon bukkyō zensho* 大日本仏教全書. Vol. 119. Tōkyō: Bussho kankōkai, 1912.
GR *Gunsho ruijū* 群書類従. Tōkyō: Zoku gunsho ruijū kanseikai, 1982.
KRN *Kōfukuji ryaku nendai ki* 興福寺略年代記. Vol. 29/2, *Zoku gunsho ruijū* 続群書類従, 107–205. Tōkyō: Zoku gunsho ruijū kankōkai, 1930.
KB *Kugyō bunin* 公卿補任. Vols. 53–58, *Kokushi taikei* 國史大系. Tōkyō: Yoshikawa kōbunkan, 1964–67.
KE *Kōfukuji engi* 興福寺縁起. *Dai Nihon bukkyō zensho* 大日本仏教全書, vol. 119. Tōkyō: Busshō kankōkai, 320–326, 1912.
KR *Kōfukuji rūki* 興福寺流記. *Dai Nihon bukkyō zensho* 大日本仏教全書, vol. 123. Tōkyō: Busshō kankōkai, 1–28, 1912.
NS *Nihon Shoki* 日本書紀. Vol. 2, *Nihon koten bungaku taikei* 日本古典文学大系 67. Tōkyō: Iwanami shoten, 1957–1967.
SN *Shoku Nihongi* 続日本紀. Vol. 2, *Nihon koten bungaku taikei* 日本古典文学大系 68. Tōkyō: Iwanami shoten, 1957–1967.
SB *Sonpi bunmyaku* 尊卑分脉. Vol. 59, *Kokushi taikei* 國史大系. Tōkyō: Yoshikawa kōbunkan, 1966.
TK *Tōshi Kaden* 藤氏家伝. *Tōshi kaden, Kamatari, Jō'e, Muchimaro den, chūshaku to kenkyū* 藤氏家伝・鎌足・貞慧・武智麻呂伝：注釈と研究. Tōkyō: Yoshikawa kōbunkan, 1999.

Secondary sources

Aston, William George, trans. *Nihongi: Chronicles of Japan from the Earliest Times to A.D. 697*. 2 vols. Rutland, VT: Charles E. Tuttle, 1972.
Andreeva, Anna. *Assembling Shinto, Buddhist Approaches to Kami Worship in Medieval Japan*. Cambridge, MA: Harvard University Asia Center, 2017.
Bauer, Mikaël. "The Chronicle of Jōe—A Translation of the Second Part of the History of the Fugiwara House." *Asiatische Studien – Études Asiatiques* 72, no. 1 (April 2018): 207–214.

Bauer, Mikaël. "The Chronicle of Kamatari: A Short Introduction To and Translation of the First Part of the History of the Fujiwara House." *Asiatische Studien – Études Asiatiques* 71, no. 2 (June 2017): 477–496.
Bauer, Mikaël. "The Power of Ritual: An Integrated History of Medieval Kōfukuji." PhD diss., Harvard University, 2011.
Bauer, Mikaël. "Tracing Yamashinadera". *Journal of Asian Humanities at Kyushu University* 5 (March 2020): 17–28.
Beck, B. J. Mansvelt. "The Fall of Han". In: *The Cambridge History of China*, Vol. 1. Cambridge: Cambridge University Press, 317–376, 1986.
Bender, Ross. "Hachiman" In Jonathan A. Silk, Ed. *Brill's Encyclopedia of Buddhism* Vol. II, 971–975. Leiden: Brill, 2019.
Bender, Ross. " The Hachiman Cult and the Dōkyō Incident". *Monumenta Nipponica* 34:2 (1979), 125–153.
Bender, Ross, trans. *Nara Japan, 758–763: A Translation from* Shoku Nihongi." CreateSpace Independent Publishing Platform, 2016.
Bender, Ross, trans. *Nara Japan, 767–770: A Translation from* Shoku Nihongi. CreateSpace Independent Publishing Platform, 2016.
Bender, Ross, trans. *The Edicts of the Last Empress, 749–770: A Translation from Shoku Nihongi*. CreateSpace Independent Publishing Platform, 2015.
Bender, Ross. "Changing the Calendar: Royal Political Theology and the Suppression of the Tachibana Naramaro Conspiracy of 757." *The Japanese Journal of Religious Studies* 37, no. 2 (2010): 223–245.
Bender, Ross and Lu, Zhao. "Research note: a Japanese Curriculum of 757". PMJS:
Premodern Japanese Studies (pmjs.org), PMJS Papers, November 2010.
Bentley, John R. *Historiographical Trends in Early Japan*. Lewiston, NY: Edwin Mellen Press, 2002.
Bentley, John R. "The Birth and Flowering of Japanese Historiography: From Chronicles to Tales to Historical Interpretation." In Foot, Sarah and Robinson Chase F. ed. *The Oxford History of Historical Writing: Volume 2: 400–1400*. Oxford: Oxford University Press, 2012.
Bock, Felicia, trans. *Engi-Shiki, Procedures of the Engi Era*. 2 vols. A Monumenta Nipponica Monograph. Tōkyō: Sophia University, 1970–1972.
Bohner, Hermann, trans. "Wake-no-Kiyomaro-den." *Monumenta Nipponica* 3, no. 1 (Jan.1940): 240–273.
Bohner, Hermann, trans. "Kamatari-Den. Taishokukwan-den. Kaden, d.i. Haustraditionen (des Hauses Fujiwara) Oberer (Band)." *Monumenta Nipponica* 4, no. 1 (Jan. 1941): 207–245.
Bohner, Hermann, trans. "Muchimaro-Den: Kaden, d.i. Haustraditionen (des Hauses Fujiwara) Unterer (Band)." *Monumenta Nipponica* 5, no. 2 (July 1942): 412–436.

Bingenheimer, Marcus. *A Biographical Dictionary of the Japanese Student-Monks of the Seventh and Early Eighth Centuries: Their Travels to China and Their Role in the Transmission of Buddhism*. Buddhismus-Studien 4. München: Iudicium-Verl, 2001.

Bowring, Richard. *The Religious Traditions of Japan: 500–1600*. Cambridge, UK: Cambridge University Press, 2005.

Bushelle, Ethan. "Mountain Buddhism and the Emergence of a Buddhist Cosmic Imaginary in Ancient Japan." *Japanese Journal of Religious Studies* 45, no. 1 (2018): 1–36.

Chan, Yen-Yi. "The Kōfukuji Nan'endō and its Buddhist Icons: Emplacing Family Memory and History of the Northern Fujiwara Clan, 800–1200." PhD Diss., University of Kansas, 2018.

Como, Michael I. *Shōtoku, Ethnicity, Ritual and Violence in the Japanese Buddhist Tradition*. Oxford: Oxford University Press, 2008.

Duthie, Torquil. "The Jinshin Rebellion and the Politics of Historical Narrative in Early Japan." *Journal of the American Oriental Society* 133 no. 2 (April–June 2013): 295–320.

Duthie, Torquil. *Man'yōshū and the Imperial Imagination in Early Japan*. Leiden: Brill, 2014.

Ebersole, Gary L. *Ritual Poetry and the Politics of Death in Early Japan*. Princeton, NJ: Princeton University Press, 1989.

Enomoto Jun'ichi 榎本淳一. "Fujiwara Nakamaro seiken ni okeru tō bunka no juyō" 藤原仲麻呂政権における唐文化の受容. In Kimoto Yoshinobu 木本好信, ed. *Fujiwara Nakamaro seiken to sono jidai* 藤原仲麻呂政権とその時代, 20–43. Tōkyō: Iwata shoin, 2013.

Gentz, Joachim. "The Ritual Meaning of Textual Form: Evidence from Early Commentaries of the Historiographic and Ritual Traditions." In Kern, Martin ed. *Text and Ritual in Early China*, 124–148. Seattle: University of Washington Press, 2005.

Gentz, Joachim. "Long Live the King! The Ideology of Power Between Ritual and Morality in the Gongyang zhuan," in: Y. Pines, P. Goldin, M. Kern eds. *Ideology of Power and Power of Ideology in Early China*, 69–117. Leiden: Brill, 2015.

Farris, William Wayne. *Japan's Medieval Population: Famine, Fertility, and Warfare in a Transformative Age*. Honolulu: University of Hawai'i Press, 2006.

Fujii Yukiko 藤井由紀子. "Fujiwara Nakamaro to nittōsō Jō'e" 藤原仲麻呂と入唐僧定恵. In *Tōshi kaden wo yomu* 藤氏家伝を読む, edited by Shinokawa Ken and Masuo Shin'ichirō, 213–245. Tōkyō: Yoshikawa kōbunkan, 2011.

Fukuyama Toshio 福山敏男. *Nihon kenchiku shi kenkyū* 日本建築史研究. Tōkyō: Bokusui shobō, 1968.

Go Tetsuo 呉哲男. "Nihon shoki to shunju kuyōden" 日本書紀と春秋公洋伝. *The Journal of Salami Women's University* 69 (2005): 1–15.

Grapard, Allan G. *The Protocol of the Gods: A Study of the Kasuga Cult in Japanese History*. Berkeley: University of California Press, 1992.

Groner, Paul. *Ryōgen and Mount Hiei: Japanese Tendai in the Tenth Century*. Honolulu: University of Hawai'i Press, 2002.

Hall, John W. and Jeffrey P. Mass, eds. *Medieval Japan: Essays in Institutional History*. Stanford, CA: Stanford University Press, 1988.

Hardacre, Helen. *Shinto, A History*. Oxford: Oxford University Press, 2017.

Hasebe Masashi 長谷部将司. "Fujiwara no Nakamaro to Tōshi kaden." 藤原仲麻呂と藤氏家伝. In *Fujiwara Nakamaro seiken to sono jidai*, edited by Kimoto Yoshinobu, 179–190. Tōkyō: Iwata shoin, 2013.

Hayashi Rokurō 林陸朗. *Kōmyō kōgō* 光明皇后. Tōkyō: Yoshikawa kōbunkan, 1961.

Inoue Mitsusada, "The Century of Reform." In *The Cambridge History of Japan*, edited by John Whitney Hall et al., 163–220. Cambridge: Cambridge University Press, 1993.

Kern, Martin ed. *Text and Ritual in Early China*. Seattle: University of Washington Press, 2005.

Kimoto Yoshinobu 木元好信, ed. *Fujiwara Nakamaro seiken to sono jidai* 藤原仲麻呂政権とその時代. Tōkyō: Iwata shoin, 2013.

Kimoto Yoshinobu 木元好信. *Fujiwara no Nakamaro: sossei wa satoku kashikoku shite* 藤原仲麻呂：率性は聡く敏くして. Kyōto: Mineruva shobō, 2011.

Kimoto Yoshinobu 木元好信. *Fujiwara no Nakamaro seiken no kisoteki kō satsu* 藤原仲 麻呂政 権の基礎的考察. Tōkyō: Takashina shoten, 1993.

Kimoto Yoshinobu 木元好信. "Fujiwara no Nakamaro no bukkyō seisaku to sōgō " 藤原仲麻呂の仏教政策と僧綱. *Komawaza shi gakkai hen* 33 (1985): 52–60.

Kimoto Yoshinobu 木元好信. "Fujiwara no Nakamaro shōron, ritsuryō kanryōsei kokka to senken izoku no shōmetsu" 藤原仲 麻呂小論、律令官僚制国家と専権遺族の消滅. In Kimoto ed., *Fujiwara Nakamaro seiken to sono jidai* 藤原仲麻呂政権とその時代, 77–88. Tōkyō: Iwata shoin, 2013.

Kishi Toshio 岸俊男. *Fujiwara no Nakamaro* 藤原仲麻呂. Tōkyō: Yoshikawa kōbunkan, 1987.

Kōchi Haruhito 河内春人. *Hendō no yochō* 変動の予兆. In Kimoto ed., *Fujiwara no Nakamaro seiken to sono jidai* 藤原仲麻呂政権とその時代, 89–110. Tōkyō: Iwata shoin, 2013.

Levy, Ian Hideo. *Hitomaro and the Birth of Japanese Lyricism*. Princeton: Princeton University Press, 2014.

Liu An. *The Huainanzi: A Guide to the Theory and Practice of Government in Early Han China*. Translated and edited by John S. Major, Sarah A.

Queen, Andrew Seth Meyer, and Harold D. Roth. New York: Columbia University Press, 2010.
Lowe, Bryan D. *Ritualized Writing: Buddhist Practice and Scriptural Cultures in Ancient Japan*. Kuroda Institute Studies in East Asian Buddhism 27. Honolulu: University of Hawai'i Press, 2017.
Mansvelt Beck, B.J. "The Fall of Han." In Vol. 1 of *The Cambridge History of China*, edited by Denis Twitchett and Michael Loewe, 317–376. Cambridge: Cambridge University Press, 1986.
Matsuo Hikaru 松尾光. *Tenpyō no seiji to sōran* 天平の政治と争乱. Tōkyō: Kasama shoin, 1995.
McMullen, I.J. "The Worship of Confucius in Ancient Japan." In *Religion in Japan*, edited by P.F. Kornicki and I.J. McMullen, 39–77. Cambridge, UK: Cambridge University Press, 1996.
Miller, Harry, trans. *The Gongyang Commentary on The Spring and Autumn Annals*. New York: Palgrave MacMillan, 2015.
Miyai Yoshio 宮井義雄. *Ritsuryō kizoku Fujiwara-shi no ujigami ujidera shinkō to sobyōsaishi* 律令貴族藤原氏の氏神．氏寺信仰と祖廟祭祀. Seikō shobō, 1978.
Miyazaki Kenji 宮崎健司. *Nihon kodai no shakyō to shakai* 日本古代の写経と社会. Tōkyō: Hanawa shobō, 2006.
Nakanishi Yasuhiro 中西康裕. *Shoku nihongi to Nara chō no seihen* 続日本紀と奈良朝の政変. Tōkyō: Yoshikawa kōbunkan, 2002.
Naoki Kōjirō. "The Nara State." In Vol. 1 of *The Cambridge History of Japan*, edited by Delmer M. Brown, 221–267. Cambridge: Cambridge University Press: 1993.
Ooms, Herman. *Imperial Politics and Symbolics in Ancient Japan: The Tenmu Dynasty, 650–800*. Honolulu: University of Hawai'i Press, 1999.
Piggott, Joan R. "Tōdaiji and the Nara Imperium." PhD diss., Stanford University, 1987.
Piggott, Joan R. *The Emergence of Japanese Kingship*. Stanford, CA: Stanford University Press, 1997.
Sakaue, Yasutoshi. "The Comparative Study of the Ritsuryō Bureaucracy in Ancient Japan and Tang China". *Acta Asiatica* 99 (2010), 19–38.
Sakamoto, Tarō. *The Six National Histories of Japan*. Tokyo: University of Tokyo Press, 1991.
Sakharova, E.B. "Kaden". Zhizneopisanie roda Fujiwara. – Orientalia et Classica. Trudy Instituta vostochnyh kultur i antichnosti. Vypusk VII. *Politicheskaya kultura drevnei Yaponii*. Moscow, 2006, pp.182–255 ("Kaden". The Biography of Fujiwara House. Orientalia et Classica. Papers of the Institute of Oriental and Classical Studies. Issue VII. Political culture of ancient Japan).
Sakharova, E.B. "Fujiwara House Biography: Continental Prototypes." *Russian Japanology Review* 2/1 (2019): 81–106.

Shinokawa Ken, Masuo Shin'ichirō ed. 篠川賢, 増尾伸一郎編. *Tōshi kaden o yomu* 藤氏家伝を読む. Tōkyō: Yoshikawa kōbunkan, 2011.

Sima Qian. *Records of the Grand Historian: Han Dynasty I.* Revised, edited, and translated by Burton Watson. New York: Columbia University Press, 1993.

Skaff, Jonathan Karam. *Sui-Tang China and Its Turko-Mongol Neighbors.* Oxford: Oxford University Press, 2012.

Sterckx, Roel. *The Animal and the Daemon in Early China.* Albany, NY: State University of New York, 2002.

Takashima Masato 高島正人. *Fujiwara no Fuhito* 藤原不比等. Tōkyō: Yoshikawa kōbunkan, 1997.

Takayama Yuki 高山有紀. *Chūsei Kōfukuji yuima-e no kenkyū* 興福寺維摩会の研究. Tōkyō: Benseisha, 1997.

Teeuwen Mark and Rambelli Fabio ed. *Buddhas and Kami in Japan, Honji Suijaku as a combinatory paradigm.* London: Routledge, 2003.

Togashi Susumu 冨樫進. "Kanshin no keifu: Tōshi kaden ni okeru gunshinkan to sono tokushitsu. 諫臣の系譜:『藤氏家伝』における君臣観とその特質." *Nihon bungaku* 56, no. 9 (2007): 1–11.

Tyler, Royall, ed. and trans. *Japanese Nō Dramas.* London: Penguin Books, 1992.

Tyler, Royall. *The Miracles of the Kasuga Deity.* New York: Columbia University Press, 1990.

Watson, Burton trans. *The Vimalakirti Sutra.* New York: Columbia University Press, 1997.

Wilkinson, Endymion. *Chinese History: A New Manual.* 2nd ed. Cambridge, MA: Harvard University Asia Center, 2013.

Yamagishi Tokuhei 山岸徳平, ed. *Kodai seiji shakai shisō* 古代政治社会思想. *Nihon shisō taikei* 8. Tōkyō: Iwanami shoten, 1979.

Yoshikawa Shinji 吉川真司. *Ritsuryō kanryōsei no kenkyū* 律令官僚性の研究. Tōkyō: Hanawa shobō, 1998.

Index

⌘

Abe no Sukunamaro, 7
Amaterasu, 3, 20
Ame Toyotakara Ikashihi no Sumeramikoto, 53
Ame Toyotakara Ikashishi Tarashi Hime, 52
Ame no Koyane no Mikoto, ix, 3, 20, 39, 40
Ameyorozu Toyohi no Sumeramikoto, 53–54
Asuka palace, 56, 67

Bo Qin, 66

Celestial Rock Cave, 3
Chang'an, 64
Chikō, 13, 18,
choku go jō, 11
chūnagon, 8, 86
Chunqiu gong yang zhuan, xiii, xvii, 46
Chunqiu, xiii, xvii, 46, 55

daigaku no kami, 7, 34, 78
daigaku no shōjō, 8
daigyō, 27
Daijin zenshi, 6
da yitong, xvii
Dharma King, 6
Dong Zhuo, 45
Duke of Zhou, 39, 66

Dōken, 55
Dōkyō incident xi, 6

Emi no Oshikatsu, xi, 13, 90
Enkei, 19, 28, 71

Fujiwara no Fuhito, ix, xii, 4, 7–8, 11–13, 15, 22, 29–30, 32–33, 39, 58, 71, 74, 86, 90, 96
Fujiwara no Fusasaki, ix, 8, 87
Fujiwara no Hirotsugu, 9
Fujiwara no Kusumaro, 15
Fujiwara no Maro, ix
Fujiwara no Michinaga, 2
Fujiwara no Miyako, 86
Fujiwara no Muchimaro, ix, xiv, xv, xvi, 7–9, 15, 19, 22–24, 33–38, 68, 71–72, 74–76, 80, 82–84, 86–87, 90, 92
Fujiwara no Nakamaro, ix, xi, xii, xiii, xiv, xv, xvi, 1, 3–29, 32, 35, 38–39, 58, 68, 71, 74, 90, 93–94
Fujiwara no Otomaro, 10
Fujiwara no Shikachi, 16
Fujiwara no Toyonari, ix, 5, 7, 8, 90
Fujiwara no Umakai, ix, 8–9
Fujiwara no Yoshiyo, 29
Fukushin, 55
Furubito no Ōe, 53
Fusō ryakki, 23
Futa-tama-no-mikoto, 20

Gangōji, 63
Gan Jiang, 64
Genbō, 9–10
Genkō Shakushō, 32–33, 64
Genmei, 78
Genshō, 10, 81
Guiji, 64

Hachiman Shrine, 6
Hannya shingyō, 18
History of the Han (Hanshu) xvii, 19, 44, 84
Hōkōji, 51
Honji suijaku 34, 35, 96
Hossō, 9, 31
Huainanzi, xiii, 19, 40, 47, 60, 61, 64, 89
Hye'un, 33
hyōbu no daifu, 10

Jikun, 12
Jinshin wars, 2
Junnin, xii, 13–17

Kae Kim, 56,
Kamitsumiya, 44
Kanmu, 2, 5
Kannon, 62
Keikō, 36
Kibi no Makibi, 9, 10, 17
Kojiki, xii, xiv, 19–20, 34, 36, 40, 54
Kong Zi, 66, 69–70
Kugyō bunin, 7, 24
Kōfukuji, xii, xv, 1, 4, 11–13, 21, 29–32, 62–63, 65, 68, 73
Koguryŏ, 56- 57
Kōgyoku, 48
Kōken, ix
Kōmyō, ix
kugyō, 7, 24
kunimi, xvi, 37, 82

Man'yōshū xii,
Min (Master of the Dharma), 41–42
Minamoto no Tamenori, 30
Mononobe no Hironari, 16
Muzashi, 46–47

Naka no Ōe, xv, 27, 28, 44, 45, 46, 48, 49, 50, 52
Nakatomi no Kamatari, ix, 3, 19, 20, 24, 39, 42, 54, 64
Nakatomi no Mikeko, ix, 20, 24
Nakatomi no Muraji, 3, 24, 54
Nihon seiki, 55
Northern Fujiwara, ix, xv, 4, 21, 38, 87

Okamoto, 42, 44, 49
Ōharae, 20

Pŏmmyŏng, 29
Prince Shioyaki, 15–16

Qibi Heli, 56

Records of the Grand Historian, xvii
Rikkoku shi, xii

sadaijin, 8, 51
Saeki no Muraji Komaro, 49, 50
Sakahibe no Omi Marise, 44
Sanbō'e kotoba, 30
sangi, 9, 87
Sataku Seimei, 63
Sekiten, 76
Shibi chūdai, 10–11
Shibi naishō, 10, 18
Shiji, xiii, 34, 46, 49, 55, 67, 72
Shikibukyō, 10, 86
Shoku Nihongi, xi, 1, 4, 5, 7, 11–13, 15–16, 35, 73, 76, 81, 84
Shōmu, ix

Shōtoku Taishi, 24
Silla, 58
Soga no Emishi, 25, 41, 44–45, 49, 51, 52
Soga no Iruka, xvi, 2, 25–26, 44, 48–49, 51–52
Soga no Ishikawa no Maro, 25
Soga no Kuratsukuri, 25, 41–42, 45–46, 51
Soga no Ochi no Iratsume, 47
Soga no Toneri no Omi, 60
Southern Fujiwara, xvi, 4, 38, 73
Spring and Autumn Annals, xvii, 19, 46
Suiko, 2, 40
Sumemi Oya no Mikoto, 53–54
sumeramikoto, 48–49, 52–54, 56–57
Susano-o, 20

Tachibana no Moroe, 5, 9, 10
Tachibana no Naramaro, 1, 11, 18
Taihō ritsuryō, 11, 13, 74
Taika rebellion, xiv
Tang period, xiv, 2, 13, 22, 77
tengyō, 27, 44
Tenji, xv, 2–3, 25–28, 40, 42, 55–60, 62, 67–69, 78, 80
Tenmu, xv, 2, 16, 57, 71, 73, 75, 78, 87
Toyomi Kekashiki, 40

Toyura no Ōomi Emishi, *see Soga no Emishi*
Tōdaiji, xi, 1, 4, 11, 13, 14, 17–18, 23
Tōnomine Ryakki, 32

udaijin, 8
udoneri, 8, 73
Umayasaka dera, 31

Vimalakīrti Assembly 12, 18, 29, 31–32, 46
Vimalakīrti Sūtra, 30, 63, 70

Waka Inukai no Muraji Amita, 49–50
Wake no Kiyomaro den, xi, 92
Wei Zheng, 56
wuwei, xvi, 37, 79, 89

Xuanzang, 64

Yamashinadera, 12, 21, 29–31, 62
Yamashiro no Ōe, 44–45, 52
Yamato Takeru, 34, 36–38, 83
Yan Hui, 70
Yuima-e, *see Vimalakīrti Assembly*
yūryaku, 27–28, 43–44, 47
Yōrō ritsuryō, 11, 13, 58

Zhang Liang, 44, 46, 61

For Product Safety Concerns and Information please contact our EU representative GPSR@taylorandfrancis.com
Taylor & Francis Verlag GmbH, Kaufingerstraße 24, 80331 München, Germany

www.ingramcontent.com/pod-product-compliance
Lightning Source LLC
Chambersburg PA
CBHW052133300426
44116CB00010B/1885